I0471021

SEVEN FIGURE MARKETER

Living The Internet Dream

DANIEL LEW

Copyright © 2013 Daniel Lew

All rights reserved. No part of this publication may be reproduced, stored in a retrieval system or transmitted in any form by any means, electronic, mechanical, photocopying recording or otherwise, without the prior permission of the publisher and copyright holder.

Daniel Lew asserts the moral right to be identified as the author of this work.

Author: Lew, Daniel
Title: Seven Figure Marketer: Living The Internet Dream

ISBN: 149094270X
Subjects: Business.

Marketing
Entrepreneurship
Sales
Internet

Title ID: 4353851
ISBN-13: 978-1490942704

http://www.danlew.com
http://www.sevenfiguremarketer.net

DISCLAIMER

All care has been taken in the preparation of the information herein, but no responsibility can be accepted by the publisher or author for any incorrect investments of time or money spent as a result of taking action from the book

SEVEN FIGURE MARKETER BY DANIEL LEW

Daniel Lew has 20 years experience in Marketing, Sales and Running Successful Online Businesses and will teach you how you can build yourself up from scratch from nothing just like he has done.

Daniel Lew husband and father thrives on teaching his students to "work smarter not harder".

Since the age of 15 he was an early high school drop out and now up until his current age of 35 he has become a self made millionaire.

This book was inspired to be written by the high end coaching program he runs and from the pure encouragement of his students.

CONTENTS

ACKNOWLEDGMENTS

A big thank you to all the IM'ers in the JV communities. But with sincerity, I honestly have only one man to thank - John Chow. He showed me the way from the very beginning.

As for the ladies; my darling wife who always believed in me. My mother, a publisher who is a savvy business woman. She inspired me to become successful and my sister Andi Lew; an Author of four books and publisher of three. You're all a big influence in my life.

INTRODUCTION

Although there is nothing wrong with the conventional nine to five office job and some people actually enjoy spending 40 or 50 years of their life in a cubicle somewhere I'm guessing that you are not one of those people. If you were, you probably wouldn't have picked up this book. The reason you are reading this book is that you too want to break free of those shackles and make your living on the Internet.

Fortunately you have come to the right place.

In this book I will run through some of the very successful strategies and tactics that I have personally employed over the course of my online career. There are many different ways that you can make money online, so it is important that you tap into the skills that you already have and find the path that best fits your particular set of talents. In this book there is a huge amount of variety and content. I have personally found success following these exact strategies and you can too.

Yes you will need to put in the work and up skill and educate yourself. But if you really are serious about breaking free of the shackles of a regular job, take note of everything I tell you and take action on what you learn here today and you too can be a hugely successful Internet mogul.

Now onto a little bit about myself…

Honestly I never thought making money online was possible. In fact there were months when I stayed up for hours and weeks where I didn't have days off because I didn't want to fall into the trap of working for someone ever again. I wanted to be my own boss and control of my own destiny.

In fact, my main motivation was being able to spend time with my beautiful wife each day. I didn't want to be away from home for ten hours a day and arrive home exhausted and frustrated with my boss or colleagues. Working from home and having the time to do what when I wanted really appealed to me. I could also spend time with my wife, doing the things we enjoy together all week long, not just on the weekends.

I wanted to be able to financially support my family and knew that making money online would give me the income and freedom to do this and be able to spend my time how I wanted without having the constraints of a job.

Originally born in Australia, I dropped out of high school at fifteen and became a self-taught Graphic Designer. Life was tough for me back then and I went from job to job and never lasted more than six months in any one of them. This carried on for almost ten years until I was about 25.

After a while I wanted to break free from sitting behind a computer and dabbled with sales to become a door to door salesman and then later a car salesman. That was all great BUT it still wasn't secure in my eyes.

Soon after I hit a massive road block in my life; I had a major car accident and near death experience. This was the catalyst for me to change direction and I decided to travel.

With the little money I had in savings and a credit card I left to go and work in the UK as a car salesman in 2003.   I really needed to break away and get out of Australia and this was my opportunity for a fresh start.

On my way to the UK I stopped over in Thailand. I was in a country that was so alien to me and although I don't know why I really went there I was just so pleased that I did because from the moment I arrived it just felt right.

It was at that time I realized the potential for buying and selling goods and had the idea that I would return to Thailand in the future and take a different direction with my life.

Once in the UK I worked as a car salesman and even though I was comfortable that I had a job I did not feel my future was secure. I needed an exit strategy and my visa was running out fast.

I received some valuable advice from my mentor at the time, his formula was very simple "Be Consistent and Don't Give Up"...

But before I was able to really achieve huge change in my life I needed to experience the process of making mistakes and learning the ropes. I needed the paint before I could create the picture.

In around 2004 I made the final decision to move to Thailand and start an Ebay business. Due to sheer determination I soon became a powerseller and business was going really. However that did not last and soon the competition became fierce and shipping goods became a struggle.

As the market slowly died down I began looking for another new trend and came up with the idea of moving into building business directories. At this point a global site called Globe Search Pty Ltd was born, and we were doing ad placements and upgrading our clients to SEO services, It was growing so quickly I had to team up with a partner and set up an office in the heart of the city with twelve staff. Life was sweet but then in 2009 the global crisis hit.....

I went back to the drawing board AGAIN! This time taking the lead from my mentor I latched onto a new trend - Affiliate Marketing. It really opened up my eyes and my specialty was traffic generation using unique SEO and blogging techniques; getting my blogs to the top of Google.

My first ever sale was when I ranked "Business.com Promo Code" in Google, I was making 2k a month just from one blog post. This offer was listed in Commission Junction and around the same time I caught onto the trend and it opened up my mind to creating even more and more posts and creating more niche sites directed in coupon codes, review sites, bonus sites and more.

I was then getting into lead generation and converting leads into sales through email marketing, but it all started with getting the traffic with SEO which is dead easy to learn once you know the basics.

Actually if you enjoy writing you can just create a simple blog using WordPress and you are good to go. Just pick a niche you're passionate about and go for it.

My first affiliate commissions were in 2009 through Commission Junction (CJ.com). I remember in my first month I made $459 and it seriously amazed me and opened up my mind to the bigger possibilities. Then the month after it was $1,572 and so on until I was easily making $300 a day. In fact my motto was if I wasn't making $1,000 a day then I wouldn't be satisfied.

I thought if only I could just rinse and repeat, the opportunities would be endless.

Around 2010 I decided to create my own products. My first product ever was 'Keyword Winner' which I listed on Clickbank. I created this product based on the amazing results I had with ranking my posts. And what better way to create a product than by using my own experience of what has worked for me. Not just some re-hashed product for the sake of it.

After that I expanded my product creation team and formed a company to pump out over twelve products. Not only for my own sites but for clients as well. We covered all areas of traffic and by 2013 I did my first seven figures ($1 million dollars) just in product creation and affiliate marketing. It was a true breakthrough.

Now at the ripe young age of 35 I look back and all of the hardships were well and truly worth it. This is what has helped me become thick skinned, and given me the experience and set the foundations to really grow exponentially from this point on.

I wanted to create this book to save you the years and years of frustrations I had to go through.

So shall we get started?

CHAPTER 1

LET'S TALK ABOUT REALITY

Life is what you make of it and I wasn't about to settle into a life of mediocrity. I wasn't going to simply go with the flow and ease myself into an existence that could be best described as nothing more than average. I wanted more than that and I knew that I had to do something about it if I wanted to achieve that goal. A better life wasn't going to just fall in my lap if I didn't do something.

There were a few things that really got me going toward building a successful Internet empire. It was a really a combination of issues, along with the determination to make a better life for myself. I had to prove to myself that I can do better and enjoy my life while I'm still young. I didn't want to put off to tomorrow what I could achieve today. I wanted to enjoy life now and not when I'm old and can't really enjoy it anymore.

To get going, you really have to find that fire in you and do some real soul searching. For me, it was easy, as I came from the bottom and worked my way up. I knew what it was like to be at the lowest of the lows. I knew what it felt like to have nothing and to feel like nothing. And it was from that day forward that I knew I didn't want to hit rock bottom ever again.

But it wasn't just about avoiding the bottom of the bottomless pit. I also wanted to have all the nice things in my life that the people around me were able to enjoy. I wanted to have those fancy cars in my driveway. I wanted to live in the big mansion with the fancy décor and high-end home theater system. I wanted more and I wanted to live in the lap of luxury. And I was determined to make this dream a reality.

I made it my mission to work hard and to work intelligently until it did happen and I can proudly say that I am leading that luxurious lifestyle now. It wasn't easy, but I got there. And now that I am here, I can sit back and simply enjoy the Internet dream, because I am now at that stage where I can only oversee everything. It's about the big picture and less about the details. Believe me: maintaining this great lifestyle has become a lot easier than trying to get here in the first place. But you can get here too. You too can enjoy this glorious way of living.

Getting back to reality, it was around the same time that I made this mission for myself that I was also seeing a direction of change with the economy. It was getting harder and harder to find work and it was getting harder to even find clients. Working for other people just wasn't working out anymore, because no one was doing any hiring. It certainly didn't help that working for someone else necessarily has its limits in terms of earning potential. I wanted more and I had to find out how to get it.

Very rarely do we get people answering their phones these days and this makes it even harder to do business. Usually, when you get to the secretary and the boss is away, the usual story is, "Can I take a message for you? I will get him to call you back." Do you think he ever calls back? Do you think you'll ever get through to him?

Another prime example is when you go to university. If you do go and you come out looking for a job, you end up spending a good majority of your time studying only to come out and work for someone else, hoping that they won't fire you tomorrow. And that's making the giant assumption that you'll get hired at all in the first place.

It occurred to me that the shift was changing quickly and if you didn't keep up with it, you would sink and fast. Who wants to live on the edge right? Its when you really dig deep and ask yourself, "Do I really want to have to wake up at 7am every morning, drive in bumper-to-bumper traffic and have to put a fake smile on my face to get through the day?" Is it really worth it? Is that really want you want out of life? Is that how you want to spend the next 20, 30, 50 years of your life?

Now the truth is you may already be feeling these things and the reason why you're reading this book in the first place is to secure your future and get an internet business up and running.

Well, you've already made the first and most important decision by picking up this book and considering the alternative possibilities to the conventional job.

My personal suggestion is if you already have a job then stick to it, don't ever leave until you make some sort of money on the internet that you know you can scale. I know this is a tough pill to swallow, especially if you're tired of your existing job and you really want to leave, but reality is reality and bills still have to get paid in the meantime. The last thing you want is to tell the man where to stick it and then watch as your internet business goes down the tube.

Be smart. Give yourself at least six months of consistent revenue online with your Internet business. When you know that your online income is going to be reasonably steady and it's enough to sustain your lifestyle, then it would be a safe bet to leave.

There are going to be a lot of people out there who will tell you that your Internet business will never take off if you leave yourself with the crutch of having a regular 9-to-5 job. They're going to tell you that you simply don't have the time to dedicate to your online business when your time and your attention are still distracted by that conventional job.

There is some truth to that, but let's be real. If you don't have enough of a nest egg to fall back on and you haven't grown your Internet business to the level where it's consistently generating reliable revenue each and every month, it's just not worth telling your boss to stick it. You still have to pay those bills and the last thing you want to do is put yourself in mountains of debt as you wait for your Internet business to take off.

But that doesn't mean you can't get started today and that doesn't mean that you can't make your Internet business a priority. In fact, that's the only real way that your online money-making ventures are really going to take off. You need to dedicate yourself. Work on your Internet business in the evenings and on the weekends. Every free moment that you have, consider what you can do to grow your online business. Learn more about what you can do and how you can make it more profitable.

And as it grows, you'll get closer and closer to that goal of having six months of steady online revenue so you can finally quit your job and pursue your Internet business full time. But it all starts with earning that all-important first dollar, so getting back to the reality of the situation, let's dive in and see how you can make some real money on the web, one dollar at a time.

DANIEL LEW

CHAPTER 2

THE AHA MOMENT

I remember my first "Aha!" moment and it's not until you get that very special moment that you can truly have faith in this business and continue to push yourself to make more and more.

You need to make it your mission to make that first dollar. Don't worry so much about your first hundred or your first thousand dollars. If you set too big or too high of an expectation and then you don't achieve it, you'll get disheartened. You'll get unmotivated. You may quit altogether and that'll waste all of your efforts and hard work.

I know people who go into the world of online business and say that they will make their first million dollars in the first three months. A lucky few might be able to do it, but realistically, that's just not going to happen. They quit and they go back to their regular jobs, never to pursue an online venture again. What a waste.

You need to be realistic. You need to be prepared to try different things and see what you feel most comfortable with. Then, you have to be prepared to stick with it, even when it might not pay off right away. This is a marathon, not a sprint. It's only when you stick with it and really learn about what works (and what doesn't work) that you can make your online business a real success.

I know people who love blogging or search engine optimization, I know others who love social marketing, and I know others who love email marketing or even video marketing. There are so many different opportunities to explore and so many different ventures to try. You need to have a passion in something and stick with it until you see results first and then move onto other things later once you see one thing is working first. Most of your efforts aren't going to take off right away, so you have to be willing to endure those slumps and slow periods if you want to enjoy the peaks and the incredibly profitable times.

Now let's say you want to do multi-level marketing (MLM) or Affiliate Marketing or maybe you even have your own product or service to sell, you need to drive the website traffic. So, regardless of which path you are taking, you will need to get familiar with the ways to do those things, but you also need to get really familiar with how to generate traffic and generate relevant traffic. We will cover that in the other chapters of this book.

For now, what I really want you to do is to really dig deep into the right mindset to be a successful Internet entrepreneur. It's not like going to a regular 9-to-5 cubicle job. You'll need to get out of your comfort zone on an ongoing basis. You'll need to learn and to keep reading other blogs and sites, absorbing all that news and free information that is available on the web to quickly see what suits you best. There's a lot of content out there, so you'll need to be careful about getting overwhelmed too. You need to find that great balance. Learn lots, but don't burn yourself out.

The moment you get overwhelmed, you need to stop take a deep breath and think about what it is that you already know and how to scale that. If you can figure out the best way to make one dollar on the Internet, the next logical step is to figure out how to do exactly the same thing, but on a much larger scale to earn ten dollars. Or a hundred dollars. Or a thousand dollars. Always think about how you can take what you already know and make it bigger with minimal additional effort.

Always go back to basics when you are overwhelmed. The best way to do this is to get away from the computer and get some fresh air. Yes, even when it comes to a business that inherently involves a computer and the Internet, sometimes you just need to step away and reset the system. The best way to open up your mind is to look outside the box. Literally.

I have found the best ideas come to me when I was either in the shower, working out at the gym or even just driving my car or before I go to sleep. That's just how the brain works. It's almost when you are thinking least about the thing you want to accomplish that you get the best ideas for how to accomplish it. Let those ideas come to you naturally.

In fact, in those precious moments before you go to sleep, your mind mind be ticking at a million miles an hour, so I encourage you to have a pen and paper beside your bed. Don't rely on your memory, because it can be awfully unreliable. I can speak from experience that I can come up with a great idea as I'm about to fall asleep and then I tell myself that I can work on it in the morning. Guess what happens when I wake up? I completely forget the idea. Don't let that happen to you.

By having that pen and paper next to your bed, you can

develop the habit of writing things down so you don't forget. Write everything down and write it in such a way that it'll make sense to you not only a few hours from now, but even a few days or a few weeks from now. You never know when you might revisit those thoughts.

If you have a smartphone or a similar device, in fact, you already have a digital pen and paper with you all the time. When you're out shopping at the market or you're going for a run around the park, you can quickly jot down those brilliant money-making ideas as they come to you. This way, you won't forget. Get into that habit.

So being organized plays a big role in helping you make your first dollar online. Once your head is clear and ideas are on paper and you are getting into a rhythm you will see yourself succeed sooner or later, it's just a matter of time.

It's not so much about how you make that first dollar online. It could be from blogging, it could be from affiliate marketing, or it could be from selling your own products or services. The most important thing is to get started, organize your thoughts, and do everything that you can to earn your first dollar from your Internet business. And from there, you can scale up, do better, and it'll snowball from there, eventually earning your first hundred, your first thousand, and yes, even your first million dollars on the Internet.

There's one more way of doing this – manifesting money. Have you ever heard about manifesting more money (or anything for that matter) in your life? This is a technique where you make use of law of attraction, thereby manifesting more money. According to experts, money flows like energy. And you can use the law of attraction to allow money flow into your life easily and quickly. But what you need to do is to connect your own subtle energy with the money current.

Many people are already benefiting from the money manifestation technique. So, why can't you? There are several tips and guidelines that you can use to manifest more money and increase your earnings very quickly.

Some of these include –

Get into the Feeling of Having More Money

According to the universal law of attraction, you'll attract those things that are always on your mind. It can be anything. It can be flowers. It can be family. It can be friends. It can be cars. Or else it can be money. If you want to make more money, you need to look at money as a friend. However, this friendship shouldn't be based upon greed. By getting into the feeling of having more money, you can activate your own subtle energy with the current of money. It will allow money to flow easily into your life.

So, what are you going to do? Well, you need to meditate for a couple of minutes every day. Imagine having more money, more than enough money. Envision it and how it makes your life more pleasurable and happier.

Be Generous

Believe it not, giving back has great power. In fact, giving back is so powerful that it can also attract more money. Make it a habit of spending at least 8% – 10% of your earnings on those who need it. Help the homeless. Lend a helping hand to the poor. It's a proven fact that the giving back brings prosperity.

Say 'No' to Unnecessary Expenses

In order to manifest more money, you should also prevent yourself from becoming a spendthrift. You need to have a healthy love for every dollar that you spend (again, it shouldn't turn into greed). Therefore, you need to take a closer look at your daily expenses and find out where you're spending unnecessarily. If you need it, you should spend money. If you only want it, you can avoid it.

Be Thankful for What You Have

When you want to manifest more money into your life, you also need to be grateful for everything that you already have in your life. Looking at the less-fortunate and the less-privileged will make you feel grateful. Being thankful for the things that you are blessed with helps you grow even more. It's all about being positive and releasing subtle energy to connect with the current of money.

Get Rid of Negative Thoughts & People

Finally, you need to believe that money manifestation works. You can activate the law of attraction for yourself only when you think positively. It's not just about getting rid of your own negative thoughts, but it's also about avoiding the company of those people who think negatively.

CHAPTER 3

THE IRON SUIT

Confidence sells. If you are not confident or you don't come off with a certain air of confidence, others will start to see these as signs of weakness. And this makes it far easier for people to slander you, take advantage of you, walk away from you, and step all over you. If you want to sell, you need to be confident. And regardless of how you choose to make your money, realize that you are selling something.

It is very important to be confident (or appear confident) in everything that you do. Are you talking on camera at an event or conference? Look confident when you speak. Are you doing a webinar or a seminar where you are trying to be perceived as the expert? You need to look confident there too. This is very important, because people don't want to buy anything from people who appear to be weak or unsure of themselves. If you are unsure of the product that you're selling, why on Earth should I be confident in buying it?

A big part of this has to do with shedding away the thin skin you may currently have and develop a thicker skin. There are going to be critics and naysayers. There are going to be people who won't believe in you or what you say, but you have to shrug them off and keep moving forward. You have to be persistent. You have to be so sure in what you're doing that you can easily convince other people.

I guess how I developed my thick skin was many years ago when I was working as a door-to-door salesman. As you can imagine, it was very hard work and the conversion rate wasn't nearly as high as most people would hope. I had to learn to deal with rejection and face each new door as a new opportunity. I had to deal with it with a fresh mind, a fresh perspective and refreshed vigor. Every door that I knocked on was another opportunity to make a sale.

Yes, it's true. It took anywhere from five to ten rejections before I was able to get one or two sales. That's hard. That's hard to swallow and hard to accept, but this is quite normal for door-to-door sales. In fact, it's quite normal for all sorts of other sales environments and businesses. Think about how many people walk into a shoe store, for example, who don't walk out having purchased a new pair of shoes. The percentage is very small, but the salesman has to remain cheerful, optimistic and confident that he will get the sale with the next customer who walks in the door. You can see how this is even more important for people who work in higher end sales, like in car dealerships and jewelry stores. Rejection is common, but confidence is persistent.

The best thing you can possibly do as a salesperson is to really know your stuff. If you really know what you're doing, then you give yourself the best opportunity for success. That's the main thing. You want to stack the odds in your favor and not throw away a sales opportunity even before you really give yourself a fair chance at it. From that point on, it just continues to be a numbers game. Get more potential customers and you'll get more opportunities to sell, fully recognizing that you might get rejected.

It's all about having thick skin and handling rejections or even worse being ignored altogether but still being able to push and move forward regardless. There will be many times where people think you are begging, spamming or even come across desperate when you talk to them about business and if they do that's their own take. Don't take it personal you just need to continue doing what you feel is right to make it happen.

Some of the most successful people that this planet has ever seen were originally viewed as being eccentric or even crazy. They faced rejection after rejection in hopes of getting funding or getting their projects off the ground. Many people said that they would never make it. And they were wrong. By having that thick skin and having that absolute conviction that what they were doing was right, they persevered and found monumental success. You can too.

You might even have some of your best and closest friends tell you that you're coming across as desperate or that you aren't going about running your business the right way. Remember whey they are friends with you in the first place and that is to do business with you. If they don't agree with you about a message regarding a cross promotion or product launch, then you need to move on. You need to find like-minded people who are more in line with your philosophy and how you want to do things. That's why you want to get into the business of the Internet in the first place; you want to do things your way. You want that freedom. You want to be in charge of your own path, your own destiny.

Let's face facts.

After all, the bigger you get, the more haters you are going to get. There are going to be people who say that you're doing it completely the wrong way and there are going to be people who are jealous of what you've been able to achieve. They have their reasons, but you have to have thick enough of a skin to just brush them off and keep doing what you're doing. The bigger you get, the more haters you will get.

This is quite normal. Think about it on a larger scale for a moment. Let's say that you're just starting out and you only have 100 followers on Twitter or some other social media platform. There's a very good chance that you have at least a few haters on there. Now, think about if you have 1000 followers. It is guaranteed that at least 5-25% of them are going be either envious or hateful. It's guaranteed. That's just how it is.

Now, look at someone like Bill Gates. He's huge. He has tons of money and he's done all sorts of things that some people may not like or may find questionable. Do you think everyone likes him? Hell no! I would at least 20% hate him and yet look at how big he is. Look at the empire that he's been able to build and look at all the philanthropic work that he's doing now. Do you think he really cares what other people think about him? Honestly? No, he has already made his tremendous mark on the industry and on the world. Who is the one that's laughing now? He is. He's laughing all the way to the bank and back to his multi-million dollar mansion.

You need to be fit for business in order to be educated in a certain profession. There are certain things that can be learned, for sure, but you have to start with the right kind of mindset and you have to be prepared to tackle the obstacles that will be placed before you. Let me give you an example.

If you want to join the army, you need to also do the core exercise training. You need to be physically fit even before you get started. And then, you also need to be prepared to do all the training and exercises related to your interest or passion in technology or science or mechanics, whichever you choose from. You need both. You need to be the complete package and you need to be prepared to add on top of that if you want to be successful. Building your online business and growing it to the point where you are making a steady and sizable income on the Internet is the exact same thing. You have to enter being fit and you have to start with the right mentality, but you have to be prepared to train and put in the work.

So, the idea behind all of this is that you need to be fully fit both mentally and physically. When you are at your highest possible level and you think you can achieve the best possible results, you need to push yourself even further. You need to push yourself to the absolute limit, right? The only way you can really discover just how far you can go is to reach just beyond what you think are your limits. Push further. The possibilities, you'll quickly learn, are actually quite limitless. You are limited only by yourself. How far are you willing to go?

Well, don't let this scare you away from the industry of making money online, but it's true. If you have a strong mind, you're willing to work and you're open to new and sometimes unconventional ideas, the other areas of learning and implementation become much, much easier to grasp and to accomplish.

You just need to start by putting on that iron suit, growing that thicker skin, and being prepared to stay steadfast in the face of adversity and rejection.

CHAPTER 4

THE PASSION IS PASSION

A lot of people will tell you that you need to have a passion about a certain hobby or area of interest before you decide to get into that line of business. Some of them will tell you that you should already have experience in that profession before you should go ahead and create a product. They might even tell you that you should have this kind of foundation in place even before you consider marketing someone else's product and making commissions from that.

There is a little bit of truth in there. It helps a lot when you are already passionate about a certain topic, hobby or industry before you decide to have it as a part of your Internet business or as part of the world of work. This way, you can stay interested in what you're doing, even when the money isn't really matching up with your efforts. If you enjoy what you are doing, as they say, then you never have to work a day in your life, right?

Not really.

My take on the matter is, sure, you could be passionate about "surfing" and you could create a blog about it. You could post every day about surfing, new surfing events, new surfing products, and everything to do with a surfer's paradise or a surfing lifestyle, but if you don't put yourself in a business point of view, then your passion doesn't mean all that much. If you don't structure the website to funnel leads and if you don't find offers or create products to sell around the site, then your passion is history.

No matter what your passion is, no matter what niche or industry you want to approach, if you don't think about how you can make money from it, you really aren't going to make any money from it. The passion about the subject helps, but the passion about how to monetize your efforts is ultimately far more important.

I like to go even one step further than that and say that if you can't create a product on "life" itself, then you really are not living. Think about for a moment. To live life is totally an amazing thing, right? If you put all else aside for just a second and think about creating a downloadable e-book on how to brush your teeth, how to take deep breaths, how to stretch or what to eat, you just might have a product right there. Let's say that you're passionate about these kinds of things. That's great. That allows you to create a viable product that you can promote and sell. And you do need to sell it.

If you can package something up as a digital product – either as an e-book, a video package, an online course, some downloadable software, or whatever else – then you have your product. Then, you have something to sell and you can be well on your way to making your first dollar, your first hundred, and even your first thousand dollars on the Internet. And once you figure it out one time, once you've done it through one time and understand what you need to do, you can repeat the cycle and scale it up to make even more money.

Does it have to be only digital? Of course not!

If you want to create a physical product that can be sold on the Internet, you can totally do that too. Maybe you might consider creating some custom funny t-shirts or some specialized equipment or some other product. If you don't have a problem with handling the orders, processing the payments, packing up the product, and shipping them to your customer, then do it by all means.

Heck, I was even a Power Seller on eBay years ago and I was able to earn a fairly sizable income selling things there. That said, the only reason why I got out of selling products on Ebay was because I didn't have a team behind me at the time that could help with inventory, logistics and shipping. Your case might be different, but do realize that shipping physical products can present some other challenges that you might not want to face and it may include some more complications when it comes to scaling up. Selling a couple products a week is easy, but try selling several thousand of those products in the same seven days.

Anyways, getting back to the real top of this chapter, the real passion is not really about the product when you boil it all down. The product, as it turns out, isn't quite as important as what you might think. Instead, the real passion is about making the money. So, honestly, if you are making money selling trinkets or widgets, then who cares as long as you are not doing any harm to someone and if you're not selling drugs or selling a product or service that will harm anyone. You could be passionate about brushing your teeth or surfing the big waves, but if you can't make money in those industries, then all of your efforts and all that passion will just go to waste.

Just pick a product or service in a booming industry and capitalize on that opportunity. Focus all of those passionate energies into making money within that niche and you'll be all the happier for it. Believe me.

Recently, I noticed a product called BioPrinting. It's a technology that effectively creates body parts based on some really sophisticated technology. The technology is still in its relative infancy and not too many people know about. It's really early on for them in terms of expansion, but the growth potential is huge. It's monumental and this creates a giant opportunity to cash in and make some serious money.

So, you can easily create something in this industry, either in digital or some kind of physical format, that you can could really enhance people's awareness of BioPrinting. Chances are that you've never heard of it and neither have most of the people out there, but you can see how it could be a booming industry and there could be a lot of interest if people just knew about it. And you can make money on this interest every step of the way.

Let's look at another example. Another thing that you might consider is, let's say, yoga. It's such a big market and it continues to grow in its followers, but yet there are very little physical products to sell around it if you compare it to a similar industry like the wide array of gym stuff. There are so many products you can sell related to the gym, but with yoga, you really only have the yoga mats. At least, that's how it appears on the surface.

When you take a step further and dig a little deeper, you can expand your mind to realize that there are actually loads of yoga-related products that you can sell to a very enthusiastic audience. You can sell stretching equipment or yoga-related clothing products, for instance, or you can even create your own stretching exercise program to sell as an info product. And let's not forget about all the tangential industries that are just as interesting to the yoga audience, like all the health and diet products that are out there. People who do yoga are very likely to enjoy health foods, because they want to be healthy. You can cross-promote and really monetize that demographic.

The best way to get passionate about any given idea or any given niche or industry is to watch those boring TV infomercials and TV commercials late at night. It might not seem like a lot of fun at the time, but those commercials can be really educational in terms of teaching you about what opportunities are available. There is a never-ending supply of health products that you can sell and, as you can imagine, these can prove incredibly lucrative. Suddenly, that research doesn't seem quite so boring, does it?

Another example of the latest fitness trend that people are getting into is called "Crossfit." Some of you may have already heard of it and it may be growing in popularity in your town, but there are a lot of people who are still new to it and really want to learn more. What is Crossfit exactly? It's basically a variety of all sports and training rolled up into one exercise program. It takes the best parts of other exercise disciplines and combines them into one very effective workout.

Well, how hard would it be to use that same kind of concept but in other parts of interest? How hard would it be for you to think about all the different products and information that are readily out there for your consumption, and the combine their best parts, their best elements into something that is even more powerful than all of the individual components combined? The key is to take those little bits of knowledge of things and form them into one, making your own product is that is unique and has something unique to offer to the consumer.

And that's really the most critical thing to remember. You want to have something unique to offer to the world, but you also have to remember that the unique thing needs to be marketable and it needs to attractive. People have to want it and that's why it helps to start your journey from one of the hottest trends or industries and then build your unique product out of that. Then, you can use mobilize your passion for making as much money as possible, combine it with the unique product, and now you've got an awesome formula that just can't be beat.

CHAPTER 5

GETTING OUT OF YOUR COMFORT ZONE

You've probably heard the saying before. You'll notice how the real successful people out there and maybe even the mentors you already have will always say this: you need to get out of your comfort zone.

The fact is that they also do this and they do this on an ongoing basis. It's not about stepping outside of your comfort zone for just that one task or just that one project. It's about having that willingness to take risks and to do things that may not feel all that easy or all that comfortable. The most successful people in this world, believe it or not, are always stepping outside of their comfort zones and this is what separates them from you, so to speak.

It's not until you really do things that you are uncomfortable with that you will really give yourself the chance to break through to the next level. If you just keep doing what you're doing and you stick with what feels comfortable, you can only hope to maintain a certain level of mediocrity. You're only trying to maintain the status quo and, chances are that you'll just end up falling behind the curve instead. Safe is boring and safe is ultimately the least safe thing you can do.

Think about that for a moment. If you keep doing what feels safe and what feels comfortable, the best you can accomplish is to stay where you are and even that is unlikely. If you want to achieve more, you have to be willing to try something new, even it makes you feel uncomfortable.

Who really likes to do webinars? Who really likes to get up on stage to talk in front an audience of critical strangers? Who really wants to trudge through and write that book when they can just as easily spend that time playing games in the park or going out to watch a movie?

They say that when they polled a group of people about their greatest fears, the fear of public speaking actually ranked higher than the fear of death. Do you realize what this means? It means that more people would prefer to be the dead guy in the casket than to be the guy on podium responsible for giving the eulogy. That's a mind-boggling fact, but it is entirely true.

Very few people actually enjoy speaking in public. Very few people actually want to take that risk of hosting a webinar or going through the struggles of writing a book, but guess what? It is exactly those people who will end up seeing so much more success, because they are the ones who are willing to do something that most people aren't willing to do.

They say that the early bird gets the worm, but there are so many birds who are too afraid to leave their nests to even go after that worm. It's just too soft and cozy and comfortable in that nest, but the brave bird who ventures out into the world really does get that worm. And the worm is one wonderful prize.

Yes, if you're willing to step outside of your comfort zone, then you have effectively given yourself a monumental advantage over just about everyone else.

There are millions of people who are ready to go to events and listen to the experts speak on the topics that they think matter. There are millions of people who are willing to pay to watch those informative webinars, because you're the one willing to put on that webinar. There are tons of people with their wallets wide open, anxious to give you their money for an online course, an e-book or some other product. And it's because so many of these people aren't willing to step out of their own comfort zones to do these things themselves. These are the kind of people who like to sit and watch people and to have a mentor.

You can be that mentor.

You can be that expert.

You can be that hero or role model type figure that everyone else aspires to be. You just have to build up that thick skin, build up your confidence, and be willing to step out of your comfort zone to do things that other people aren't willing to do.

When you overcome your fears, you can then reap the rewards. In fact, even if you don't necessarily make any real money from hosting those webinars, doing those conferences, publishing those books or putting together those online courses, it doesn't really matter too much. You will make money if you stick with it and keep plugging away. It will surely happen and all of those pieces can serve as the foundation to your long-term success.

And that's the thing. You have to look beyond the immediate future when you think about stepping outside of your comfort zone. It's not about making a quick buck, because things can change tomorrow. Instead, by having all of those products under your belt and by building up all that valuable experience, you are working toward associating yourself with a brand, a strong brand, because people like to buy from people.

As you develop more of these kinds of products, you will become better known in the niche or industry of your choosing. People will start to recognize that you are the go-to guy or go-to gal for any information related to yoga, to Crossfit, or to whatever else that you choose to promote and grow. You are your brand and people like to know that you are a real person. Real people like to buy from real people and all that effort you put into building your personal brand helps to build up your presence in the marketplace. People will come to know you and trust you.

You know what? You also get to be seen as an authority in your niche almost instantly when you take the risk and when you do the things that are unexpected.

The people that go with the flow and follow all the crowds just end up getting lost in the crowd. They become the wallflowers that no one really notices, because they're not doing anything different. They're not sticking their necks out and taking a risk. They're blending in. If you step outside your comfort zone and really put yourself out there in front of the world, then you'll be noticed. Then, you'll be the expert. You'll be the trusted authority and it is with that branding, that trust, that you'll be able to be able to develop and sell even more products.

And make more money. And isn't that what it's really all about in the first place?

Let me give you another prime example of this. I never used to write. I didn't feel particularly comfortable with it and it really wasn't something that I really wanted to do, but you know what? I pushed myself not only to do it, but to keep getting better at it. I forced myself to get the message out there that I wanted to get out there, because if I didn't do it, who would?

Come on, do you think that if I hired someone else to write for me that my message would really come across the same way that I wanted it to come out? Would it really still sound like my voice? Would it really convey the meaning of what I wanted to get across? No way. No chance.

I had to do it myself, even if it was a really hard thing to do. And believe me, it wasn't easy, but I'm so glad that I pushed myself to do it.

I'm so glad that I pushed myself to do something that didn't feel all that comfortable to me, but I knew that the rewards would be all that much more rewarding if I did it myself. And I knew that it would be far more authentic and true to what I wanted to say.

Another great example of this is networking and meeting people in the same niche. Many of us can be socially awkward, it's true. It can be tough to meet new people and it can be hard to spark up those casual small talk conversations with total strangers and it can be even harder to gear those small talk conversations into something more substantial or something more relevant to what you want to accomplish. It's one thing to just say hi and politely nod at someone. It's another thing to really forge a strong business relationship that is mutually beneficial.

It's starts with putting yourself out there. And that can be even more challenging depending on where you live and work. Myself, I had to fly and make those investments to go to seminars and conferences so that I would have the opportunity to meet people. If I didn't do that, there's no way I would be where I am today. The investment of paying for the flights and hotels and all that more than covered themselves, because I got to joint-venture (JV) with people that I wouldn't have been able to otherwise.

If I didn't make those connections, if I didn't get the chance to work with those success-minded people In the same kind niche as me, I would not be able to accomplish what I have. I'd still be sitting at the same old desk, trudging away at something that might not have gotten anywhere on its own. You need to network. You need to connect with other people. You need to get out there and really take chances.

In case you didn't already know, I'm Australian, but I didn't just stay put. Moving to Thailand and even working in the UK was totally out of my comfort zone. There were some brand new cultures with different ways of doing things, different food and different people. I had to leave behind the friends and family that I knew. I had to leave behind the home that I knew. I had to leave behind the familiar city where I knew everything that I needed to know, venturing into places that were completely unfamiliar.

But if I didn't do those things or make those big steps, I definitely would not have ended up where I am today. Those experiences helped me grow as a person and they really helped to open up my perspective to the rest of the world. I learned. I got wiser. And I have been able to apply that experience to the things that I do today. They made me smarter and more well-rounded. And I don't mean to say that to sound self-centered or conceited or anything like that. Traveling the world and living in foreign lands really does open up your eyes.

Heck, I know some people who are so scared to do anything out of their normal way of living that they haven't even left their own city, let alone their own country. Can you imagine that? Never leaving your own town, never getting on a plane, never going out there to really see and experience what it's like in the rest of the world? How can you possibly understand how to market and sell your products to an international audience on the Internet if you've never even ventured beyond your city limits?

These people, they are even too afraid to make new friends, hanging around the same people all the way through childhood until they're old and withered. Guess what sort of life they're able to lead? Unsurprisingly, they tend to lead a very average life, because they didn't open up their minds to new opportunities. They were too afraid to try something new. They were too scared to take a chance and step outside their comfort zones.

Let's be real. The more opportunities you have, the more you can grow and be associated with the right crowd. Network with your mentors and elevate your game as a result.

It's all about positioning. You ain't going to be positioned correctly if you don't ever move, right? It's only logical.

Here is a series of photos of me meeting some of the experts in the industry as a result of networking and guess who's the expert or considered the guru now as a result of networking and being associated with other experts? I am! ☺

- Anthony Aires and Brad Gosse: Bottom Left (USA event)
- Aaron Darko: Top Left (Thailand)
- David Cavanagh: Top right (Thailand)
- George Brown and Tom Miller: Bottom Right (Australia)

CHAPTER 6

HELL TO THE NAYSAYERS

You've probably heard the same old story from your friends and family. Don't tell me that you're of those people who take on board exactly what your parents tell you to do. If we all did that, the world would be populated with nothing but doctors and accountants who are prim and proper in everything that they do.

Don't get me wrong. It's important to respect your parents and listen to what they have to say, but you shouldn't just accept their preferences and their directions for you as gospel. You're not a puppet. You are your own person and you have every right do whatever it is that you want to do with your life. I mean, seriously, this is probably why you are where you are today. You tried to make them happy, but you just ended up making yourself miserable in the process.

You never listened to your own real wants and wishes. You never pursued the things that you really wanted to pursue and that's why you might find yourself stuck going down a path that didn't really interest you in the first place. It was just to make them happy and they're still not happy. Let's face it: it's just not worth it. At some point, you just have to put yourself first and really do what you really want to do.

Yes, sure, it's important to be open to what your family has to say and what they want, but remember that the views of your parents, uncles, aunts and grandparents are usually outdated. They're from another generation with an entirely different world view than the one that you have. Things change and we all have to learn to change with them. Their views just might not be in compliance with what you want. And that's why you have to take that leap of faith and stick to your guns.

The fact of the matter is that if you have a gut feeling about something, you really need to go with it. You can't really spend all that time trying to justify your decision or figure out a way to explain to your friends and family why it is that you want to do what you want to do. It might not even make perfect sense to you in the beginning, but that's okay. If in your heart of hearts, you have that gut feeling that this is a good idea, you have to give it a chance. You have to give it a try.

If you don't take that chance and follow through on your gut feeling, you will forever feel sorry that you didn't do it. This will play on your mind for years to come and no one wants to live with that kind of regret. You don't want to look back years from now and wonder what could have been. You don't want to leave any stone unturned, especially when you really think that particular stone is worth exploring and turning over. You have to look. You have to try.

Other people might say that you are foolish. Other people might say that you are crazy or that endeavor is an utter waste of your time, but you know what? They're wrong.

No matter what you choose to do, no matter how you decide to make your riches on the Internet, you're going to encounter so many haters and naysayers along the way. They won't believe you and they might not respect you, but you need to follow through on your dreams anyway. I'm sure that many people thought Steve Jobs was crazy for trying to take on Microsoft and the PC world, but look at where Apple is today. Lots of people probably thought the guys behind YouTube, eBay and Facebook were pretty nuts too, but those are some of the most successful websites on the Internet today.

It's because they took a chance. It's because they allowed themselves to ignore their opponents and cast aside the naysayers, focusing on what they really believed in and what they really needed to do to succeed. Perhaps more importantly than all of this, they unwaveringly believed in themselves and what they wanted to achieve. And this is despite having all sorts of people tell them that they're stupid or that they're destined for failure.

Trust me. I get it all the time and you will too.

It's so important to stay strong and to think for yourself. You have to do what your heart's desire is, because you definitely don't want to live with that regret. You don't want to live your life for someone else or just to follow the passive instructions of someone who isn't you. This is your life at stake and your life is completely what you make of it. Above all else, you have to listen to yourself.

Listen to your heart more. Maybe you want to try to do some meditation to be in tune with your own thought process. Take that time to look deep within yourself and really decide not only what you want to get out of life, but how you think you'll be able to get there. It is only by listening to yourself that you'll be able to make wiser decisions on your own. You simply can't let yourself become reliant on other people or what other people tell you to do.

If people have a go at you, let them. If they detract from your goals and your plan to get them, let them. They can think and feel whatever they want, as long as you stay steadfast and go with your gut. You are already confident with your own path and that's all that really matters.

You know what happens when you start focusing on factors outside of yourself? If you are the kind of character that needs to reach out to five different people before making any sort of decision, you will never get anywhere. You can't be constantly seeking that reassurance or that validation from others, because you'll inevitably encounter people who are going to be counter to your views, your goals, and your chosen path. Whether or not they intend on doing it on purpose, they'll get in your way. And you'll just get stuck where you are.

To get anywhere, you have to take those first bold steps on your own. You have to believe in yourself and what you want to do.

Why? Because everyone will have different opinions on just about everything and you will never find any sort of real consensus when you start asking everybody for what they think you should do or how you should do it. So, it's really obvious that you're not going to come up with any kind of suitable solution, when any solution is going to have its detractors and its naysayers. Someone is always going to say no. That's why you really need to connect with your own deeper intuition.

Don't be afraid to get to know yourself on the deeper level.

People are going to ask what you do for a living. Whereas other people might have more conventional answers like saying they're a teacher, a plumber or a cook, you can have a different response, because you are different. As a joke, you can respond by saying, "I sell dreams."

That's a real conversation starter, because they'll naturally follow up by asking what exactly that means. You can go on to explain what it is that you do and, bam, you just might have a fantastic networking opportunity to grow your online business. It's true that you shouldn't listen to the naysayers, but there's still definitely value in networking.

Or, the best one that I like is saying, "I am semi-retired."

Do you know why that's a great answer? There are a couple of reasons. First, usually they don't have a response back to that other than, "Oh, that's nice." Second, and this is really related to the first, is that deep down, these people are going to be thinking, "Hmmm... I want to know more about this character." They might even be jealous of the lifestyle that you're able to lead, because they're still grinding it out working the normal 40, 50 or even 80 hour week at a dead end job that leaves them coming home tired and unsatisfied.

Saying that you're "semi-retired" can make you far more interesting, rather than just saying that you "work from home" or that you're an "entrepreneur." Those statements might be just as true and just as accurate, but they are a bit broad and boring. I don't know about you, but I would rather be broad and interesting.

CHAPTER 7

BE SELFISH WITHOUT BEING SELFISH

The worst thing you can ever be is Mr nice guy and do websites or business tasks for your family for your friends and end up with no time for yourself to do your own ventures.

Time is money, money is time. And remember family and friends expect everything for nothing. You have to be selfish in a good way and be firm and strong and explain what you can and can't do or things will get out of hand and months and years will go by where you say to yourself.. It seems I still haven't got ahead.

Do you know who is always going to be on your side? Do you know who will always have your own best interests at heart? Do you know who's still going to be there, regardless of how much or how little success you are able to achieve with your online ventures and exploits? There's just one person: you.

Have you ever noticed that it's usually the good guys who get screwed? There's a saying that good guys finish last, and while that might not exactly be the fairest of situations, it's actually really close to the truth. You know the guy that passes up the promotion, because he wants to be polite and kind to his co-worker, even if that co-worker is less qualified and less deserving of the promotion? That's the guy that will perpetually be stuck in mediocrity, drifting along somewhere in the middle, never giving himself the opportunity to rise to the top.

This is the guy that steps aside so someone else can take the lead. This is the guy who will never stick up his hand when he's at an event and the speaker asks who wants to win the big prize. This is the guy that just doesn't get the most out of what he really can get, because he's too afraid to take it. He's too scared to put himself first or to stick his nose out to stand out from the crowd.

Have you ever watched Dragons Den or Shark Tank on television? Those five wealthy "dragons" or "sharks" are looking for some interesting and lucrative investment opportunities, but they aren't going to be particularly nice about it. Business isn't about being nice; it's about making money.

These venture capitalists, these investors are ruthless as hell. They don't sugarcoat the truth for the entrepreneurs when they make their pitches, because they just speak the cold, hard, honest truth. They give you a chance to prove that your product, your service or your idea is worth their investment and you only have a few minutes to do it. If you can't sell them on it right away, you already lost. If you don't prove it to them quickly, they'll slander, slam and insult you. They'll put you down quicker than you can possibly imagine.

I've watched too many episodes where the pitchers didn't have a strong grasp on what their product was all about, why it was revolutionary, or what was its unique selling proposition. They couldn't explain why their product was better than the competition and why a customer would choose to buy from them rather than the next bloke down the street. And then so many more of these entrepreneurs didn't have a strong grasp on their numbers, unable to explain how much it costs, how big is the market, what is the market potential, and how much money they can make. They had no plan, no vision.

Would it be fair to say that the dragons and sharks are selfish? Probably! They don't care if that entrepreneur goes bankrupt and doesn't get the funding that they need to bring their project to the next level.

All the dragons care about is whether they'll get a good return on their investment. All they care about is whether they can use their money to make even more money. From the get-go, they have their own interests at heart and they have every motivation and every right to feel and to act that way. How do you think they got to where they are today? How do you think they amassed their fortunes?

So, regardless of whether you like it or not, people are going

DANIEL LEW

to be selfish. Everyone else is going to be self-interested and focused on that age old question: what's in it for me? This is particularly true when it comes to those people who are already successful and they usually won't even give you the time of day to listen to your problems or questions. They just can't be bothered, because they don't have nearly as much to gain out of that interaction as you would.

This is life. This is reality. This is the truth. You can't expect everyone to want to help everyone else in this world, because that's just not how it's going to be. It's a tough pill to swallow, but the sooner you realize and accept it, the sooner you can go ahead and put your own interests at the forefront too. Be selfish. Care about what you want and how you want to get it.

The truth is that nobody can really see this. So few people are even going to notice that you are being selfish or personally driven, because it's just accepted as being the norm. By the time they realize that you are acting out of selfish interests, you will already be at the level where you are making the millions that you have always dreamed about.

Believe me. Every second of your time is positively critical, because every moment is precious. The time that you waste away procrastinating or working on things that don't matter could be far better dedicated to pushing your own agenda and moving your business forward. The decisions you need to make have to be precise and they have to be quick. If they are not and you are not being as precise and as fast as possible with those decisions, you will end up delaying your progress so badly and you will fall behind, project after project. You really have to stick with it and keep your nose to the grindstone.

It's not like we were born into this world and then we were all given some sort of handbook that explained how are you meant to do things. Life isn't that simple or that straightforward. It's way more complex than that and, more importantly, we were all given the power of free will. We have the ability to choose our destiny and what we want to do to get there.

It's up to us as humans to do the things that we need to do in order to succeed. We have the ability to choose, but we also have the responsibility that goes with it. We get to choose, but we must also understand that we are responsible for the results that follow. You might not be able to control everything, but you can choose how you handle any given situation. You can take a different path if you want to. You can do things differently if that's what you want to do. It's unfortunate, but we don't even learn the basic business skills we need when we're going through school. These are the skills and knowledge that we need to get out there and to really combat the real world.

So, the onus falls back on you again. You have to decide that you want to learn and educate yourself. You have to choose that you want to develop your business skills so that you give yourself a far better chance at achieving your goals. It's entirely up to you and that's why you are entirely justified in actively selfishly to get there.

Now, I am not really saying that you should be some selfish

jerk that is mean to people for no reason at all. I'm not even saying that you should elevate yourself to the same kind of selfish level that we see demonstrated by the rich guys on Dragons Den and Shark Tank. The fact of the matter is that you haven't earned your right to be that way yet.

When you are big and you can go ahead and sit back, looking from the top of the world instead of up at the rest of the world, you can be the one who calls all the shots without inhibition. Until then, the advice is actually pretty simple: be selfish, but be selfish in a good way!

CHAPTER 8

YOUR WORTH IS WHAT YOU PRICE IT

For many years, I made the horrible mistake of under-pricing my products. I guess you could say that I was afraid of scaring off the potential customer with a bigger price tag and I figured that making a little bit of money from that customer was better than if the customer walked away and bought nothing at all.

It's a very common fear among just about everybody who sells just about anything these days. You're scared to price yourself out of the market. You're scared to ask for too much money, because you're scared of losing out on that precious sale. But is this fear really all that warranted? Is it really all that justified? Are you really maximizing what you could accomplish with your products or services at the price that you set them today?

If I really priced those products in my early days at how much I thought they were really worth, can you even start to imagine how much more money I would have made? Can you even start to fathom how much cash I simply left on the table when it was right there for the taking? Think about how much more money I could have made long-term, but also how I could have helped to set the industry at the level at which it deserved to be and at the level where it deserved to stay?

Competition is such a devilish thing. You'll very soon realize and notice that as soon as you set your price a little lower, immediately your competitors will start to drop their prices too. In order to stay competitive and make sure that you are still able to attract those valuable customers, you respond in kind and start lowering your price some more. It's a vicious cycle and, before you know it, everyone is selling at just $1. That's not good for anyone and we are all just leaving the money on the table.

It does take a certain kind of person to stay headstrong and to keep prices higher and stronger in the face of such competition. It can be hard to resist that temptation, because if you see that everyone else is selling a similar kind of product or service for less money, you may be worried that people are going to leave and stop buying from you.

You'll notice this concept in the property industry, for example, and this is why some cities in the world still have a very strong economy. There are some cities out there where real estate is still very expensive, even if the industry in the area is self-inflated. It doesn't matter. That's beside the point. If people are willing to spend more money, then you have every right to try to earn more money from them. And this is better for everyone involved in that same industry too.

If you don't back down in price, then all the other properties won't either. The customer will see the industry as being strong and that the prices must be justified if everyone is keeping their rates high. As soon as you lower your price on your property, you're effectively showing desperation and the customer can recognize that too. It's like how some animals can smell fear. They can smell that you're desperate and you're willing to lower your price, so they might even try to negotiate your price even lower. They know you're willing to discount it. They know you're desperate for the sale. If you lower the price and show that desperation, everyone else follows. Remember, people are like sheep, so they will inevitably follow.

I remember the days when I stayed headstrong in a country where I was foreign and didn't speak the language. I stuck to my guns, despite the odds looking like they were completely stacked against me. Here I was, keeping very high prices like $10,000 for website development, while there were some other local agencies in the area that were only charging $1,000 for the same kind of work.

The thing is, it would only really be a worry to me if the customers were in comparison mode or if they were shopping around. I stuck to my guns, because I valued what I was worth. I priced my website development services at a level where I felt it belonged and my customers were better able to understand the value that I was bringing to the table. I wasn't going to short change myself and attempt to compete on price when I knew those other agencies weren't the same as me. They didn't get it. And it helped that my customers didn't necessarily know about these other agencies either.

If you were certain that they were going to get the services done through you regardless, then staying strong on your price with your head held high would always be the way to go. They might try to negotiate and they might try to knock you down a few pegs, but that's when you have to stay strong and really sell why you're better and why you're worth what you're asking for. If you stick to your guns, then nine times out of ten, they would order anyway. That's how it was with me and that's how I really recommend you go about doing things too. It's better for the industry and it's way better for your pocketbook.

Show confidence. Show value. Demonstrate your quality and support and people will be prepared to the price you want, no matter what the cost may be. People buy into confidence. If they get the feeling that you are absolutely confident in the work that you do and you're positively confident that you will deliver on all of your promises, then they'll open up their wallets and gladly give you their money. That's what you want.

Whether I charge $5,000 or $10,000 for coaching, there really is not much difference in gap between the people who will buy. You would think that with double the money, the people who may have paid at the $5,000 level would get turned off by having to pay more, but the fact of the matter is that, usually, if they are prepared to make a $5k investment in what they want to accomplish, a few thousand more is not much different.

What if they don't have the extra money on hand? That's not a problem either. You can give them payment options to work with if they need them. Giving options is very important, so you can capture as wide a demographic and as large a customer base as you possibly can, all while charging top dollar for your products or services.

For example. Option 1 could be one time payment of $247, or Option 2 could be $97 x 3 months.

Believe it or not, people are willing to pay. They just have to be convinced and they just have to believe in what you have to offer. Again, this comes back to your perceived sense of confidence and the value that you bring to the table. If they're willing to spend $5k, they're probably ready to part with more if they think they are getting more out of the deal.

Here's another great example of thinking outside of the box. You've probably seen a ton of affiliate offers on the Internet for this program or that product where they are offering affiliates an incredible 100% commission on sales. How on Earth are these companies able to make any money if they keep giving away these 100% commissions?

Well, there's a bit of a trick involved. They're not making any money on that front-end sale, that much is true. However, what most people don't really notice is where they are making the real money. The real money is being earned on the back-end. They might sell that front-end product for only $9-$47 and they might give the affiliate the full 100% commission on that, but now they have a customer who has bought into the system and is far more likely to buy into other related follow-up products and services. And those are usually for more money and they're usually continually sold over the long term. That's the real money.

You see, companies and affiliate products that say that they will give you 100% commission, you have to know that they are basically just in need of fresh leads. Better still, because they're getting the affiliates to qualify these leads by forcing them to generate real sales – so there is no reason why you can't do the same even if you give them 100% commission on that front end sale – it means that you are getting some great warm leads. These are not only customers who are prepared to open up their wallets; these are customers who have already opened up their wallets. It's not that they want to spend money; it's that they already have. That's a very high quality lead.

And from there, you can get some serious coin on the back-end, so you can keep funneling customers through into something else. It's well worth making just a little bit on the first sale to then later get them paying for more once you give them a taste, you can easily generate hundreds or even thousands of dollars from that same customer over the long haul when they like and trust what you offer them.

DANIEL LEW

CHAPTER 9

DON'T BE A WUSSY AND BLOG

At the very least you should blog post, if you don't you're being a wussy. If you can post on Facebook or tell people about your stories in person than you can blog post, in other words anyone can blog post. Its free and it's a great way to get a website up quickly with content and network with other bloggers.

Now apart from getting your blog setup using a free platform called Wordpress.org let's talk about what elements you should consider when writing content.

How to Make Your Website Content Irresistible

Is the content on your website irresistibly attractive to the target audience?

No matter how hard you try, promotion alone can't build a thriving audience for your website. In order to win the online marketing game, you should first have a closer look at the quality of your content. Unless the content on your website is truly irresistible, people won't like to share it with others or visit again.

It's irresistible content that can set you apart from the competition quickly and help you achieve success with your website.

Irresistible content is that which your audience doesn't only want to read but also loves to share with their friends or contacts. But how does content become irresistible?

Well, it all begins with the knowledge about the target audience. You should be crystal clear about who you are writing for. When you know who you are going to address and what their needs are, you'll create better content. While beginning to write the content for your website, you should know whether you are writing for college students, entry level professionals, single moms, self-employed people or career changers. When you know this, you'll get started right.

What's next?

Yes, there's a lot more. Apart from focusing on the needs of the target audience, you'll also need to follow some key steps. Here are the important ones –

Be Brave

May be, other people are already thinking about an issue or a topic, but they lack the courage to talk about it. If you make yourself brave enough to talk about it, you'll be able to attract attention instantly. No doubt, it will make your website content irresistible to others.

Use Different Formats

If you are truly serious about creating irresistible content, you should try to create content in as many different formats as possible. Videos, infographics and PowerPoint presentations attract readers visually. By leveraging the power of the visual, you can easily make your content irresistible.

Give Away Secrets

keep your secrets to yourself. The point is to help your target audience in a genuine way. Unlike others, you should feel free to give away some of your most valuable secrets with the intent of helping the audience. Your effort will be appreciated and rewarded excellently well.

Share Solutions

The target audience is actually looking for solutions. They are looking for someone who could provide quick solutions to their problems. If you are aware of solutions that have worked well for others or for you, you should go on to share them with the readers of your website.

Answer User Personae Questions

Another powerful tip to create irresistible content for your website is to answer some of the most important questions that your audience has in mind. Q&A sites like Yahoo Answers and Quora are good places to make yourself aware of the questions that relate to your niche.

Though social media sites like Facebook, Twitter, LinkedIn and Google Plus are powerful tools to promote content, you won't be able to make a hit unless your content is irresistibly attractive to the target audience.

Are You Experimenting with Different Blog Post lengths?

It's a good idea to experiment with different blog post lengths and discover what works best for your business and your target audience.

For many people, the topic of 'blog post length' is still a conundrum. They look at a short post of 300 words, and are amazed with the kind of search engine and social popularity it's got. Then they look at a blog post which is around 1,000 words long , and yet not as popular. Again, they come across a blog post which contains 2,000 words and has got hundreds of social shares. Then they locate a 600 words long post, which seems to be just perfect.

They're confused!

If you ask an SEO professional about the perfect length for a blog post, they will suggest anything between 500-600 words.

Many professional bloggers will suggest you write blog posts as long as containing 1,000 or 2,000 words. On the other hand, business professionals (who are busy like heck) would prefer keeping it short, 200-300 words.

The truth is this – 'there's nothing like a perfect blog post length. No matter what niche your blog caters to, you can't just stick yourself to a fixed blog post length and keep writing.

Many times, you'll notice a short post doing just fantastically well, much better than your longer posts. That's why you should never set parameters for optimum length. Most importantly, you should never measure the value of a blog post by the number of words it contains. Some topics will be easy to explain in just 200-300 words while others will take as many as 1,000 – 12,00 words.

It depends on what topic you're writing.
That's why blog post lengths would always vary.

Every blog is different, in terms of niche, content focus and style. The best idea is to experiment. By experimenting with different blog post lengths, you'll be able to understand the needs of the target audience or readers, what's best for your business and what's best for the chosen topic.

So, are you experimenting?

Let me tell you this experiment is also going to be an interesting and learning experience for you. So, what are you going to? Well, you can start writing some short blog posts, a few long posts and a couple of normal posts. Then you need closely watch the result or impact of each one of them. Such an experiment can prove to be an eye-opener for you.

While you start to experiment with different lengths of blog post, don't forget to lose focus on the other vital aspects. While writing a blog post, regardless of its length, you should make sure it's accessible to mobile device users as well. In addition to that, you should ensure it's appropriately formatted to enhance readability. Always focus on communicating your message in a clear and concise manner. You should always take a holistic approach towards writing better blog posts.

Are you abiding by a fixed blog post length? If yes, it's time to start experimenting with different lengths (short, long and normal) and see the kind of impact each of the sizes make on the audience.

What Google 'Likes' to See in a Blog Post

Do your blog posts have all those ingredients that Google likes?

Better blog writing is something that a passionate blogger should continue to focus on. Readers' requirements change with time, as they mature. The blog writer has to consider several aspects while crafting a post so as to make sure it's liked (and shared) by as many readers as possible. Every time, you write a new blog post, you should be able to strengthen your relationship with the reader, without whom your blog is just lifeless.

That's all good.

But, apart from focusing on the needs of the readers or the target audience, you also need to ensure that the content you feature on your blog is liked by major search engines like Google as well.

Here's what Google likes to see in a blog post –

Google Likes Text

First and foremost, you need to understand that Google loves to see a good amount of text in blog posts. If you think publishing only 100 words or 200 words long post or filling your posts with only images can help you achieve higher rankings in Google, you need to think again. Though there's no fixed length for writing a blog post, it's always a good idea to write at 400-500 words long post. In addition to that, you should experiment with different post length to identify what works best.

Google Likes Formatting

Definitely, writing quality content is the most important factor. But it's also vital to format your blog posts in a way that they can easily communicate the message you want to deliver. Whether it's the title of the post, the headings, subheadings or the paragraphs, they should all be well-formatted. Well-formatted blog posts offer ease of reading for users. That's exactly why Google likes posts with good formatting. So, don't miss it.

Google Likes Freshness (and Originality)

There are three major reasons for which Google likes fresh and original content. First, it wants to improve the experience of the user. Second, it wants to refine ad retargeting. Third, it needs fresh content to create artificial intelligence (AI) graph. If you were not paying attention to freshness till now, it's about time you started to take things into perspective.

Google Likes Outbound Hyperlinks

One of the most important traits that a passionate blogger

should possess is generosity. Linking out to other sites doesn't go down too well with many of the bloggers out there. Since Google's goal is to improve the experience of the user, it wants bloggers to include outbound hyperlinks, the only condition is that they point to authority sources and are relevant for the reader.

Google Likes Accessibility

Making your blog's content accessible is also extremely important. Only creating top quality content is not enough. You should also ensure that it's easily accessible to all segments of your target audience. Make sure your blog's content is accessible to mobile device users. Also remember to include social media sharing buttons and ensure that the commenting system that you use is friendly for users. Even the images that use in your blog posts should include descriptive text using the 'alt' tagging.

Google Likes Expertise

Expertise is one of the most important factors that matter with Google a lot. You should be aware of the latest developments regarding Google AuthorRank.

It's a new feature that helps Google to tie a piece of content or write-up with the content creator. The goal is to provide high rankings to those articles, blog posts or content pieces that have been created with experts. It's a clear indication that Google likes experts and expertise. If you want to improve your blog, you must be able to prove yourself as an expert in the niche you belong to.

While writing a blog post, you should always focus on those ingredients that are liked by Google. Unless your articles or write-ups carry the above mentioned features, it will be almost impossible to rank your blog post at the top of Google search results. Start to improve your blog's SEO from today.

A Direct Visitor to Your Blog is Like a 'Friend in Need'
Are you getting enough direct traffic to your blog? If not, this is what you must know ..

There are different sources from where traffic comes to a blog or website. Traffic to your site can come through search engines. It can come via social media platforms like Facebook, Twitter, Google+ or YouTube. Visitors can also reach your site through blog comments where you have left a link. But there's one category of traffic or visitors that doesn't need to travel along a path to reach the destination (i.e. your blog).

They don't need to use a source to land on your site because they know you or your brand already. And they really like you.
Yes, I'm talking about 'direct visitors'.

Direct visitors don't come to your blog or website through search engines or referrals. They will simply type the URL in their browsers and visit your site right away. Or they have perhaps bookmarked your URL. But one thing is sure that they associate with you or your brand really well.

Have you ever wanted to find out how much direct traffic your site is attracting? If you have Google Analytics already installed on your site, you can simply go to the dashboard, then go to 'Traffic Sources' and click 'Overview'. The data that is presented will show you the distribution of different categories of traffic that your site is getting. Direct traffic percentage is also there.

Getting a good amount of direct traffic to your site is very important. It really means a lot. In fact, a direct visitor is like a 'friend in need'. They are the most loyal of all visitors. Direct traffic is the best among all the traffic types. There are definitely various good reasons for this.

Direct visitors are the best because

- They know you, your blog or your brand really well.
- They think of you genuinely.
- They are not dependent on an outside source.
- They are likely to be the most targeted traffic.
- They are loyal.
- They can be the most responsive buyers.

DANIEL LEW

Direct traffic, as you can see, is the best form of traffic for several reasons. The best thing about these visitors is that they won't leave you even when search engines or referrals are not sending you any traffic. Even in the wake of a search algorithmic update (which resulted in a drop of rankings for your site), your direct visitors will keep coming. They will be with you!

That's why I look at a direct visitor as a real friend or a friend in need. I would really love to have more and more of them. But increasing the number of direct visitors to your blog is not as easy as you may think.

Here are some of my tips

* Focus on building a strong brand
* Set your blog apart from others in your niche
* Try to be remarkable
* Use an easy-to-memorize domain name
* Advertise through promotional items or products
* Organize live events or workshops
* Get interviewed on TV, radio

Getting more and more direct visitors to your blog is all about marketing and promotion. It's about building a brand around your blog, in a way which allows people to associate with you quickly.

CHAPTER 10

RANKING AND BANKING

In order to get a good flow of traffic to your website it's a good idea to get your sites ranking in top position in the search engines for certain keywords so you can convert those visitors to buyers. If you don't want to get involved with the technical side I suggest you hire an SEO agency that can do this for you.

Hiring an SEO Agency (or Consultant) is Not Child's Play!

Are you sure you have chosen the right SEO agency or consultant to work with?

Choosing an SEO agency that's worth your money needs some homework. Considering the large of number of these agencies or consultants out there, it becomes extremely difficult to pick one that knows their stuff really well, and that suits what you are looking for the best. The sad part of the story is that every SEO firm that you come across with will claim to give your website or blog top search rankings, whether they are able to do it or not is another matter.

So, you can be in big trouble.

Though you can't avoid the need of working with an SEO agency to improve the rankings of your website, you'll certainly need to do some homework so that you are in a better position to select the best option for yourself.

Before you go out looking for an SEO agency or consultant that can help you really well, the first thing you need to be clear about is your budget. If you do some research, you'll come to know that SEO services can cost you as little as $100 per month or as much as thousands of dollars per month. If you have a strict budget, you will definitely not want to go for an expensive option and burn a hole in your pocket. Therefore, it's important to know your SEO budget clearly well. In any case, you shouldn't have a mindset of hiring the cheapest, as it may not always be the best.

The next big thing that needs careful attention is goals. If you don't know, SEO has many different types of applications. Depending on your specific requirements, you may want your hired SEO agency or professional to do one of these.

Drive traffic to your website or blog

- Increase the sales of an e-commerce store
- Bolster your brand's authority and recognition
- Generate leads
- Manage your online reputation
- Build backlinks for your web property

Since there are so many applications of SEO, you need to be sure about what goals you are actually looking to fulfill. Before hiring an SEO agency, therefore, you should know what you will want them to do for you. It is only when you know your goals really well that you will be able to let the SEO firm know what you want and help them develop a strategy that works best.

Finally, it's time to conduct some background check. Even if you are fully aware of your budget and goals, you won't be able to hire a good SEO agency or consultant. That's why you should pull up your socks to do some screening before you finally decide to work with a search engine optimization firm.

Here are a couple of key questions you can ask

- How long have you been working in the SEO industry?
- How do you keep yourself abreast of the latest SEO developments and trends?
- What keyword research techniques do you use?
- What tools do you use to keep track of SEO campaigns?
- What kind of reporting do you offer?
- Can you give me names or contact details of a few of your satisfied clients?

Before you sign on the dotted online, you shouldn't forget to have your questions answered. By asking the above mentioned questions, you'll be able to make a better decision about whether an SEO agency or consultant you want to work with will provide great value for your hard-earned money.

Last but not the least, it's also a good idea to educate yourself about the basics of SEO so you can distinguish between what's good (white-hat) and what's bad (black-hat). So, keep on learning. There's plenty of literature on this topic you can use.

What's 'Conversion-Oriented' Link Building?

First of all let me tell you Google bases a lot of their algorithm weight on how many quality links you have pointing to your site from other authority sites.

So now that you understand that let me talk about link building with "Conversions" in mind.

Do you build links to drive conversions? If not, find out how you can..

Have you ever heard about conversion-oriented SEO? Well, great SEO is not just about improving your site's search rankings in SERPs. But it's also about increasing the rate of click-through when your site appears in search results. If no one clicks on your links in search results, what benefit are you getting from SEO? Likewise, link building can also be conversion-oriented.

Links are not just for enhancing your blog's or website's search engine rankings. But you can also build links in a way that generate conversions.

If you have an online business, your main goal is to generate more and more revenue. That's why it's important to keep your mind focused on maximizing the rate of conversions. Most of the web property owners or SEO professionals, however, use link building only for the sake of getting better rankings in search engines.

So, now is the time to fine-tune your link building strategy!

The best idea is to invest in a link building strategy that gets you better search rankings as well as drives more conversions.

To get started with conversion-oriented link building, you need to gain a deep insight into your site's statistics. Thankfully, you have Google Analytics at your disposal. By using this free tool effectively, you'll be on your way to gain a better understanding of your link building campaign and enhance the same for better results.

So, what do you do? Well, you need to start setting goals in Google Analytics. You can create several important goals in this regard. Some of these include URL destination, visit duration, pages per visit etc.

In addition to that, you can also have a thank-you page on your website. A thank-you page allows you to know whether a visitor completed a transaction or not after visiting your site. Setting up such goals will definitely give you a better insight and you would be able to make your link building campaign conversion-oriented so you can generate more revenue.

By studying the Google Analytics data of your site closely, you can also find out which of the links send you more leads or generate more conversions. By checking out Referrals under Traffic Sources, you can identify the high performing links and adjust your link building campaign accordingly.

Depending on your specific requirements, you may have different goals like getting traffic, increasing the number of subscribers, downloading an e-book or generating leads for your online business. If your goal is to attract more traffic to your website or blog, for example, you can build links to achieve the same rather than creating tons of links that may or may not improve your search rankings.

A good link building strategy is to point your links to a dedicated landing page rather than the homepage of your site. Since the landing page has a specific purpose, that traffic that you send there can be converted easily. If you are really serious about conversion-oriented link building, you should start paying attention to setting goals in Google Analytics. For many, this is a weak area. But with more practice and some expert help from outside, you'll be on your way to obtaining success.

CHAPTER 11

AFFILIATE FORENSICS

One of the biggest and potentially most profitable ways to make money on the Internet is through something called affiliate marketing. Let's start with some really basic background information, so that you understand how it came to be and how exactly it works.

In the very early days of the Internet, advertising on the web was still a very new idea and the advertisers went about it the same kind of way that they went about considering traditional media. In other words, they might approach what they feel is a high traffic or a popular website and ask if they can place an ad banner on the site. This is the same as the company asking to put an advertisement in a newspaper or magazine, or the same as buying a radio spot or having a TV commercial. This was based on a flat fee. The advertiser might pay $1,000 to have a simple banner placed on a site for some period of time.

As the technology and industry evolved, though, so did the advertisers. Instead of just paying a flat fee to place an advertisement on a website, they wanted that advertisement to perform. So, they might offer a payment on a CPM basis. This stands for cost per thousand (M means a thousand in Roman numerals, like how C means a hundred and L means fifty). Basically, they'd pay based on the number of views that the ad banner got.

So, for example, maybe they'll negotiate a rate of $10 CPM. If the page where the banner was placed was view 100,000 times in a month, the website owner would then earn $1,000 that month for that ad. That's $10 x 100. If the ad was viewed 200,000 times, the website owner would earn $2,000 and so on.

Eventually, advertisers wanted even more. Just having the ad banner seen wasn't good enough, because they wanted web visitors to click on the ad and actually visit their site. At that time, the CPC (cost per click) model was born. They might pay $1.00 a click, for example. So, if in that month, from those 100,000 views a total of 1,000 clicks were generated, the website owner would then earn $1,000. This gave the advertiser better proof of performance.

And it was from this that eventually affiliate marketing was born. We went from a flat rate, to a view-based system, to a click-based system. With affiliate marketing, the web visitor has to not only see the ad and click through on the ad, but they also have to perform a certain predefined action in order for the webmaster (or affiliate marketer) to earn a commission. That sounds like a lot more work, but you know what? It also means a lot more money. Whereas the advertiser might only pay $1.00 per click, they might be willing to pay $100 or more for what they call a conversion.

And that's where we are now. In order to make money online using affiliate marketing strategies, it's important to have this basic background information as your foundation. Then, you need to know what affiliate networks are paying in terms of commissions and how they are paying. They're not all the same, so it's important for you to learn exactly how each network or each offer is structured.

DANIEL LEW

Before we talk about the logistics of all this, let's talk about the different types of affiliate marketing that exist today. In general, the world of affiliate marketing has become synonymous with what is called CPA or Cost Per Action. But it's not all the same and the "action" part of Cost Per Action can come in a bunch of different forms.

One way that you might have already seen CPA in action would be something like an online survey. As the marketer (that's you), you would post a banner or a link to a survey online. You don't get any money directly for posting that link on a per view or a per click basis. Instead, you only get paid when a web visitor completes the "action" of completing the survey. That's one example. The advertiser is willing to pay for this, because they want as many people to actually finish the survey as possible and not just have a bunch of people click to the link and then leave without doing it.

A common subset of CPA marketing is something called CPL. That stands for Cost Per Lead. With this, you get paid when a web visitor completes a certain form on the advertiser's website. Some of these forms can be really simple, like just asking for a name and email address, or the form might ask for a zip code or some other snippet of information. The advertiser wants that lead and they're willing to pay for it. The "lead" could also take on the form of signing up for a mailing list or a newsletter of some kind. It really varies from advertiser to advertiser.

Some forms with CPL can be a lot longer, like what happens in the world of payday loans or credit card applications. With these, the web visitor might have to complete the full application form before you get paid the commission. When there is a higher barrier to entry like that, the payout is usually quite a bit higher. There are credit card companies that will pay hundreds of dollars for qualified leads, even if the applicant doesn't end up getting or using the credit card at the end.

The goal for you, then, is to send as much qualified and

relevant traffic to the advertiser's website as possible so that you can provide them with as many qualified leads as possible that actually complete the target action. From there, the advertiser might keep the lead for themselves so that they can sell that person additional products or services. Or, the advertiser might turn around and sell that "warm lead" to another company so that they can earn an even bigger commission. You only get paid for that initial action.

One network that you can consider if you want to do this CPA or CPL type marketing is peerfly.com. They're really big and they have a pretty strong infrastructure, making it easier for affiliates to do what they do to make as much money as possible. You can sign up with them, check them out and see what offers you want to promote.

The other most popular form of CPA-based affiliate marketing is based on sending a user to a direct offer page, which then requires a point of sale directly on that sales page. Not surprisingly, this kind of affiliate marketing is called CPS or Cost Per Sale. You might also see it listed on different networks and through different vendors as PPS (pay per sale) or CPO (cost per order). Basically, it's advertising where you make money when the visitor follows through and makes a sale with the advertiser.

How these pay out can vary from advertiser to advertiser. With some offers, they pay you a flat rate for referring through a completed sale. In that case, they might pay you $10 or whatever if you send them a customer that buys something on their site. Another way that they might structure it is with a percentage of the referred sale. That's how the Amazon Associates program works, which is one of the most popular affiliate programs on the Internet today.

With that program, the base level commission starts at 4%. So, for example, if you send over a web visitor who goes ahead and buys $1,000 worth of stuff from Amazon, you earn $40. That's just the base level. Amazon offers a higher and higher percentage for more successful affiliates. These are the people who are sending a larger volume each month.

Some of the most lucrative CPS affiliate marketing that you can do is when you find an advertiser that offers a monthly subscription or a SaaS (system as a service). With these kinds of affiliate programs, there is sometimes an option to earn recurring commissions for however long your referred customer stays on board.

Let's say that they offer some kind of online business software where they charge a company $100 a month to use their service. And let's say that this advertiser offers a recurring 10% commission through their referral or affiliate program. If you send over a customer who signs up, that means you not only earn the $10 commission (10% of $100) from the initial sale, but you can earn a $10 commission every month by referring that one customer. You can see how this very quickly adds up. It's the affiliate marketing model used by popular mailing list provider Aweber, for example.

When it comes to these Cost Per Sale affiliate programs, you can see straight away what conversions you are getting and what price of a sale you are sending them to right off the bat. This helps you figure out just how much your traffic is worth and how much money-making potential you have right now. That's really useful data, because it gives you the chance to tweak your marketing plans and campaigns to improve your conversion rate, improve the average size of the referred sale and so on. That's how you make more money and that's why we're all doing this!

There are hundreds, even thousands of products on the Internet that have affiliate programs set up. Just about anything that you can think of, some company probably has an affiliate program for it. In the cell phone accessory industry? Zagg has a pretty good program for the Invisible Shield line of screen protectors and other protective material. Like to dabble in home entertainment? There's an affiliate program for Netflix too. Just about everything and everyone has an affiliate program.

If you want to find if there's one in line with what you want to promote and monetize, there are a couple of strategies you can try. First, go straight to the provider or the company's website and look around for something that says "affiliate program" or "referral program." Sometimes you can work directly with the company through these kinds of programs. Another way to do it, as simple as it may sound, is to go to Google and type in the name of the product and then "affiliate." Sometimes companies use third-party services to manage their affiliate programs.

Alternatively, one of the more convenient ways to do your affiliate marketing is through affiliate networks. This is because you can then gain access to many different offers from many different advertisers without necessarily having to apply for and manage each account separately. This also means that you can combine your commissions into a single payout, rather than waiting to reach the threshold with each individual offer with each individual advertiser.

A couple of affiliate networks that I like to use are Clickbank.com and CommissionJunction.com. Sign up with them to view their marketplaces. There are people selling just about everything through there, so you're bound to find something that you want to promote.

CHAPTER 12

MLM THE DEVIL'S DREAM

Not that many people like to talk about multi-level marketing (MLM), because unfortunately, it has created a really bad name for itself over the years. Well, that's not really fair to say.

The problem is that many unsavory characters have taken to MLM and they went about doing things in a dishonest or misleading way. People have been screwed and scammed out of their money through pyramid schemes and that's why MLM has left a bad taste in the mouths of so many people. Don't let that deter you. There may be some rotten apples, but there are some really awesome pickings too.

The fact of the matter is that multilevel marketing works. It really does. MLM is very ethical if you are not getting involved in selling something that is not there. That's what you would call a pyramid scheme. That's where you really sell people into buying into a hierarchy or structure that only really pays the people at the top of the pyramid and it needs more people to keep paying in from the bottom to sustain itself. That's when people aren't really selling the product that they say they are. That's a pyramid scheme and it always collapses under its own weight. That's not multi-level marketing.

You can get based on a per-referral basis and then there are programs where if your referrals tell their friends and get more people to sign up, then you earn a commission too. You get paid from their down line and this is perfectly normal. This encourages the affiliates or members or whatever you want to call them, this encourages them to keep getting more people to sign up and to help promote the actual product or service being sold.

Some people say this sounds dirty or sneaky, but think about even how conventional business works. Let me give you an example. Let's say that there is a clothing company that prints a line of fashionable t-shirts. That's the parent company. They sign a contract with a distributor who will then buy up batches of these t-shirts to sell to other customers. The distributor might then sell the t-shirts to a wholesaler and the wholesaler might sell to an importer and the importer might sell to a local retail store and the retail store finally sells it to the final customer.

When the customer buys that t-shirt, everyone up and down that stream is getting a piece of the pie. The retailer earns the difference in price between what he sold the shirt for and how much he paid the importer for the shirt. The importer makes a cut, the wholesaler makes a cut, the distributor makes a cut, and of course the actual t-shirt company makes a cut too. Everyone gets paid, but the people closer to the top can have better earning potential, because they can have more people in their downstream. The distributor probably sells to more than one wholesaler and the importer probably sells to more than one retailer, and so on.

In fact, when you talk about multi-level marketing and the idea of being paid for the referrals that your referrals are bringing in, this is actually pretty similar to modern day affiliate marketing programs and networks. There is not much difference, as there are tons of 2nd tier programs put in place, but that's where the buck usually stops. When you get to the 3rd tier, the original affiliate doesn't make a cut anymore. But with MLM, these levels can be unlimited tiers and that's where the real difference comes into play.

I used to be a reseller for a company called Multisoft.com. We had an office in Thailand (Remember how I wrote about taking risks and expanding your horizons? That's how I ended up in Thailand and how I gained all sorts of valuable experience from my time there) and it was from there that we basically sold MLM-based software to local businesses. It was okay, but we intended to expand throughout Asia to make even more money.

It seemed like a great idea, because there were so many markets we wanted to hit and there was a lot of earning potential for these untapped markets. Unfortunately, it was a very hard one to crack, because Asia just was not ready for it at the time. It was too different of a concept for them and they weren't ready to take the plunge. They didn't want to wrap their heads around it.

Now, with so many people aware of the benefits of multi-level marketing and how much money they can make from getting

DANIEL LEW

involved with it, MLM is expanding at an exponential rate. It's blowing up and everyone is getting on board. That's great for people in it too, because it means that there are so many people who also want to join.

You just have to look at how big Empower Network has grown in such a short time to see that. There is a core product there – the blogging platform and the different modules and related products that go with it – but there is huge earning possibilities through the referral MLM network. That's why people are flocking to it and that's why people are making so much money from Empower Network. Pure Leverage is also another big one. There is some really big money to be made here if you go about it the right way. Don't let the stigma of MLM turn you off from these kinds of opportunities.

On the other hand, let's say that you already have your own product that you want to make as an MLM program similar to those networks. Can you still capitalize on this same rising trend? Absolutely! That's when you would need to create your own MLM system and you can use something like Multisoft to do that. It's totally possible.

Other than that, it is still quite a huge job to take on. Also, if you want to run your own payment system rather than running it through some other service provider, then you need to be an authorized e-wallet merchant and you need to pay out your members and you need to provide stats and all of those other things. That's a lot to handle and it's a really big task. Not everyone wants to take on that kind of responsibility and that's why it's easier to use an existing payment and tracking system that works right out of the box. These will cost more, but the convenience is sometimes worth it.

But, if you really are ambitious in the MLM industry, then you can start off with promoting other MLM offers first. This helps you get a better understanding of how everything works, what sort of promotion methods are effective (and which aren't) and how the whole system works together. It's a lot to learn and experience will be a great guide.

After you've had some experience with MLM and understand how it goes, and if you think that this is something that you want to continue doing, then you can take it further later on down the track. You might even do the MLM thing with one of your own products or services, but that's entirely up to you and it's not something that you would want to even consider when you're first starting out. It'd be way too overwhelming.

MLM also requires some networking and contacting your downline members. You even have to educate some of them, because they might be new to MLM or the system. For some, this is a bit more work than your regular affiliate marketing efforts and just sending traffic to an offer and selling. But, if you spend a bit more time with your customers in MLM, training them personally on how to do things, the rewards can be huge, especially if they have a good network. If you recruit them and then they sell to their massive email list or followers, you'll then have an army in your downline in no time.

From there, it can become a very hands-free business in the long run, generating a consistent flow of passive income for you. That frees up your time to pursue even more interests and make even more money. That's the biggest appeal of MLM.

CHAPTER 13

UGLY ON VIDEO?

Let's get one thing straight, right off the bat. No, you are not ugly, so stop being all paranoid about it. And even if you are, who cares?

Honestly, when we see that there are so many videos of people with no legs or no arms getting a million likes and shares, does it really matter how you look like? Really, it's never about how you look, it's much more about what you do that can make the difference to someone's day. People want something they can latch onto. People want someone that they can trust.

Getting on video is not an easy task, I know. A lot of people can be incredibly camera shy, especially when they know that the video is going to be posted on the Internet and potentially thousands of people are going to watch it. But that's what you want when you produce a video. You want it to be seen. You want it to be popular. You want it to build your brand and further improve your earning potential as an Internet entrepreneur.

Absolutely, doing these kinds of videos can be outside of your comfort zone, but you'll remember what I said in the chapter about stepping outside of your comfort zone. It gives you the advantage, because so many other people are scared to do it. It gives you that leg up against the competition, because you're doing something that they're too afraid to do. If you spend the time engaging with video, the self-branding and relationship you build with your audience can be much bigger than what it currently is. Video has huge potential.

If you spend the time getting good lighting and sound, if you have a good camera and put together content that people want to see, the rewards will pay off this initial investment in no time, I guarantee it.

You have to remember that the other thing is it's not just about the video itself; it's the capabilities of traffic going viral as a result of using video effectively.

For example, with the technology now available you can add opt-in forms within the video itself and collect leads. You can even add video sneak previews on pre-sell pages and as a way to entice visitors to get on your list on a squeeze page. A picture tells a thousand words, so you can imagine what a video tells, especially with the sound and visual effects if you want to get really creative. You can have a real impact.

In fact, many people when they think about blog posts, they think that their content has to be just handwritten all the time, but it's not always the case. Think about it. If you incorporate video, particularly YouTube videos that you can easily embed within a blog post, you can effectively double your traffic and this also helps to optimize your rankings in Google and YouTube. They have a certain algorithm in place to help with this.

It's important that you treat your YouTube channel the same way that you would treat your website or blog. You have to make sure that your videos are properly optimized for search, so that they are more easily found by people who are looking for videos to watch on YouTube. Make sure that your video title is enticing and descriptive, for example, and you want to make sure that you are using the right relevant keywords in your description and tags. These are the keywords that you want to rank for.

Having a website is one thing (and it's a great thing), but having an active YouTube channel is another thing altogether. If you have lots of active subscribers on your channel that are always getting notified on your new videos, and then you combine this onto your other feeds so your audience knows when you publish it, this becomes an excellent extra source of traffic that you wouldn't otherwise have gotten.

Here's something that most people don't realize. Most of us know that Google is the biggest search engine in the world, but do you know what is the second biggest? It's not Bing. It's not Yahoo. It might surprise you, but the second biggest search engine in the world is actually YouTube. What this means is that if you rank for your target keywords on YouTube, you have the potential for generating way more views than if you ranked for the same terms on Bing or Yahoo!

That's huge for branding, especially if you're using videos the right way. That's why what you put in your descriptions are so important, not to mention that you can make some money directly from your YouTube videos, as well as the indirect revenue that you can earn from posting videos on YouTube. Video is huge and it continues to grow.

The other cool thing is that you can actually add links and banners on your YouTube channel for even more brand awareness. So again, here is an opportunity for you to get more traffic, build more links, and increase your branding. You really can't go wrong.

CHAPTER 14

HOW TO SELL ICE

There is an ice factory on the highway in Burleigh, QLD Australia that has been in business for 30 years, I'm telling you either their ice tastes bloody good or they are just well connected and know how to sell, because one would have to wonder, how the hell could you make money from selling ice, right? It's just ice! There's no money in that, right?

Now let's take this same analogy and sell ice in the Sahara Desert, see how something that seemed like nothing much of value scaled even higher because it turned from a want to a need. When you make something seem like someone needs something rather than wanting then you can really make the perceived value even higher once again.

And let's say in Australia where ice is being sold in bags for BBQ's or day trips as more of a want and at say around $5 a bag. I'm sure if we could go to the Sahara desert we could sell ice for any price we wish, $100 or $1000 and people would pay for it.

Well, the same question can be asked for selling $1 products.

How the hell do those guys make money with such little return? They're selling products a dollar at a time with such a slim profit margin, so how is it possible that they are making any kind of real money at all? The real truth and where people usually fail to understand is it's not about the price of the product; it's about getting the best possible return on your investment.

It sounds simple enough, but it might take a second to wrap your head around it. Because, just like in your industry or my industry, if you come across as an authority on the subject and you provide as much quality content as possible to your audience, when it comes to selling something, believe me, they will be begging you to be sold. They want to buy from you, because they trust that you're the guy to listen to.

You also have to consider all the other factors that come into play when a customer considers the value of a product being sold. Let's go back to the example of the ice factory in Queensland. Or rather, let's just talk about selling ice in general. It's not really about the ice itself. It's also about how you package it.

So, if you have a cheap wrapper for that bag of ice, you will most likely only get a small amount of money for it, because it becomes less appealing to your potential customer base. But, if you have a gold wrapper and you put some nice packaging on exactly the same ice, you can most likely sell the ice for more money. People perceive there being a better quality or a better value inside, because it just looks like it's worth more money.

I have launched products in the past and teased them through pre-launch and people have said, "Just give me the buy button!" No joking! Honestly, when you build your audience up to a stage that you provide value over and over again, then you have already sold yourself. So, whatever you want to sell at that point becomes extremely easy. They're hooked and they want more. They've already decided that they like what you have to offer, because you've already demonstrated that you offer some real quality that they really want.

I remember back in the old days when I used to go door-to-

DANIEL LEW

door selling cable TV of all things. I used to literally walk up to the door and when they answered it, I would ask, "Do you have the kettle ready?"

It may sound strange and it may sound a little off-putting at first, but what I really meant to tell them was that it was quite cold outside. However, this ended up being a great way to break the ice. Instead of the usual "Hi, how are you?" kind of greeting that they were normally used to getting, I quickly said something else to shock them and to get their attention. This snapped them out of the automatic response that so many people have with door-to-door salesman and that was to tell them they're not interested, slamming the door in their face. I didn't want that. I wanted to get the sale. And that had to start with getting the customer's attention.

Did it work? Well, let's just say that I ended up being the best salesman of the year and it was all because of my personal tactics. These were strategies that other people didn't use, because they were too used to following the formula. They didn't know how to sell ice.

It's all about tweaking and defining your own strategies, whether you're talking about what you do online with your Internet marketing or what you do offline with something like door-to-door sales. You just need to do something to stand out from the crowd. Don't be afraid to take risks. That's how you get your competitive advantage. You have to come up with a way to be different from all the other people who are trying to sell cable television. And you have to get your customers in that kind of position where they'll even listen to what you have to say. You have to start there.

Everyone on the sales team used to be shocked when I would come back to the office at the end of the evening and I sold more than any of them. They kept on asking me, "How did you do it?" Of course, I kept my secrets, but I'm sharing them with you now. I want all of you to have the same kind of success. I want you to know how to sell ice, not only selling it better than anyone else selling ice, but even better than people selling anything else. The same philosophy applies to selling everything.

SEVEN FIGURE MARKETER

CHAPTER 15

SOCIAL SLAPPER

The web is way more social today than it was in the early days and it has really expanded the scope of what you can do on the Internet. Usually with social marketing, you are really expected to be a goof. Well, what I mean to say is that this is where you can really express your true character and be who you really are, because after all, this is a more personal you and what you're up to type of engagement that you can have with other users.

Facebook is a prime example of where you can say whatever is on your mind, regardless of what it might be. People can respond by siding with your opinion to get on your good side. This can help you bond and form a great relationship. Or, they can totally ignore you. It doesn't matter, because you're doing what you can to stay front and center on their minds. That's brand exposure and that's great for your long-term success.

The good news is that you don't have to post all kinds of pretty pictures to your profile to have engagement. In fact, as funny as it may sound, the uglier your photo, the more response you will probably get. That sounds interesting, right? Well it is. People get attracted to disgusting things and you'll find it is way easier for them to strike up a conversation based on being silly, stupid or just a plain slapper. They want to have fun and that's a great way to engage.

Regardless, social media continues to mature more and more. Whether you are known brand or a small home-based business, participating at social media actively can pay your great dividends. However, the competition is tougher and the online users are smarter than ever. As we plan our social marketing strategies, we need to focus on increasing the efficiency for a better ROI.

Given below are 5 key tips that you should abide by to get the most out of your social media marketing efforts.

1. Don't Ignore Google+ Anymore

Around 625,000 people join Google+ everyday. The +1 button is used as many as 5 million times a day. Whether you are an online marketer, an affiliate marketer or an online business owner, you can't ignore Google+ anymore. Whether you want to reach out to your target audience or increase traffic to your website or blog, joining Google+ has become mandatory in the future of marketing.

Therefore, create your profile on G+ right away and set up your business page. In any case, don't forget to visit popular company pages to find out how they are making the most of their time on Google+.

2. Go Visual

Prepare yourself to leverage the potential of quality images. Images or pictures, provided they are of superior quality, attract instant attention on social media platforms and create engagement among the audience. Whether you are a small company, home-based business or a web property owner, you must find ways to create quality images and use the 'visual power' to drive social momentum.

Social platforms like Pinterest or Instagram are excellent options when you want to share attractive photos or images with your target audience and obtain maximum benefits for your business or brand.

3. Take Good Care of Mobile Device Users

The number of mobile device users has increased at lightning speed. First of all, you need to check out the details of mobile traffic to your website and blog. Depending on what you exactly need, you should then make your web property easily accessible by users of different types of mobile devices.

No matter where your audience is at a given point of time, they should be able to easily access your website or blog. Don't miss it!

4. Fine-Tune Your Social Media Profiles

Also remember to devote some time to evaluating your

profiles on different social media profiles particularly Facebook and Twitter. Have a closer look to make sure the information that you have on each of your social profiles is up-to-date, fresh and engaging. At the same time, ensure they are optimized for organic search appropriately.

5. Work Out an Effective Content Strategy

To achieve success with social media marketing in 2013, you also need to pay close attention to the kind of content strategy you create. With the competition continuously increasing, it's vital to create content that addresses the day-to-day needs of your target audience and that's worth sharing. Along with this, you need to schedule the content efficiently as well to gain maximum reach.

CHAPTER 16

PRODUCT CREATION SICKNESS

I remember the first product I created was based on my experience I had from making money through getting commissions and ranking my pages to the first page of Google. I walked the talk and didn't just create a product for the hell of it. This is very important, particularly in the beginning of your product creation career, as people can smell from a mile away whether you have created a product for just a quick buck or if you're in it for the long haul and created a product based on where your passion lies.

There is a very common misconception out there that the only way you can make money on the Internet with your own products is to release new products on a very frequent basis. I've seen some people try to pump out a new e-book, plugin or course every month and then they wonder why they haven't been able to enjoy the success that they had hoped they would.

Don't fall into the trap of thinking that you need to create product after product. Don't become one of those product creator sickos. It will seriously burn you out and you won't even reap the rewards from all that wasted effort. I have been there, I have done that, and I can honestly tell you that no money in the world is worth risking your health. In fact, it may not even be the best strategy for making the most money possible from creating and selling your own products either.

As a matter of fact, the smarter marketers on the Internet usually only have one product launch a year. If you can hit it big the first time you do this, then all the best to you and I take my hat off to you. But you have to position your launch perfectly, really take your time setting out pre-launch building buzz and prepping your affiliates and customers for months and also having the highest of quality video and sales page to stand out from the rest.

The best products you can create are the recurring ones, because that way you get paid monthly over and over again without necessarily having to put in any extra work. As an added bonus, affiliates absolutely love promoting these kinds of products, because it provides them with residual income. Passive income really is the best kind of income.

If you do decide to get into the product creation business for yourself, just make sure that you are an expert in all the other fields that we've discussed in these chapters. Honestly, if you are weak in a certain area, you might miss something and end up doing a lot more harm than good on a launch. This hurts not only your performance on that one product, but it can hurt your brand in the long term and put a serious dent in your long term possibilities. Embarrassment is an understatement and the last thing you want to do is upset your affiliates. If they're not happy, they won't come back. They'd rather promote someone else's products.

Yes, you can launch products without having affiliates going around promoting it for you, but I don't recommend that you take on this strategy unless you really are an expert in other areas of marketing. Then, it might be okay, but you'll still face your fair share of struggles. When you have affiliate working for you, they're able to cast a much wider net and reach a much wider audience than if you tried to do it on your own.

It's true. Using affiliates really is the best form possible for getting free traffic to your products and to your landing pages. Obviously, you need to vie them a commission to help promote your product, but that's a small price to pay for vastly increasing your sales potential. It's better to have a far larger pie that you split with your affiliates than to be stuck with an extra tiny pie that won't even satisfy your own appetite.

But how can you get these affiliates on your side? Where can you find the affiliates to help promote your products? Well, you can use marketplaces like JVzoo, Clickbank or Clicksure to list your product and put up a commission rate. Another way that you can go about it is to host your own affiliate program, such as idevaffiliate. That's something to consider, but you may have a harder time reaching the right affiliates and convincing them to promote your product. At the end of the day, though, you really have to make sure you concentrate on creating quality products. If you create something that is unique and different and network to the right people sooner people should promote.

However this is not always guaranteed, remember I said "should" there is actually a big BUT in this industry and almost like a catch twenty-two. Most of the affiliates out there especially the bigger ones work off the concept "you scratch my back and I'll scratch yours". For example If you have not supported these affiliates in the past it will be very hard to get their support when it comes to your launch especially if you are new to the field.

So what you need to do is mail other product launches regularly before launching that way if you get on leaderboards people will recognize your name and when it comes to launch day for your product I can pretty much guarantee they will support back because they want to keep you as a long term JV partner.

If you are in the "make money niche" for example you can check out jvnotifypro.com or muncheye.com for the upcoming launches to promote.

However if you don't have an email list to support others then I suggest you do SEO, Social Media, Blogging or buying Solo Ads, anything to create a list quickly.

Getting back to creating products as such, if you have dozens of poorly organized online courses that teach people this or that, you're probably not going to do very well. If you have one or two excellent online courses that are really useful and that people genuinely recommend to their friends, then you're going to be a lot more successful. That being said, if you are relying on mass product creation as your whole business, you are heading for disaster.

The way I see it is like this. Launching products is really just a way to get more fresh buyer leads and to funnel them through to your other products and services. It's not about getting that one sale that one time. Get that one sale, but use it as a way to generate even more sales with your existing and growing library of other affiliate products and services. If you don't have your own products yet, you can still use this funnel to promote other products and services.

The problem with creating products is that its not like it used to be. Years ago, you could sell an ebook for $97 no problem, but now they are next to nothing. Software is slowly becoming the same way, because there are too many pieces of software that can do the same thing. More and more competition is coming in, so software devalues itself in price in order for competitors to give themselves a competing edge.

But there is one thing they cannot duplicate and that is YOU. You are the shining star and someone that cannot be duplicated, so again this comes back to building your personal brand and getting people to buy from you because they like you. If you stick to this concept, you can't go wrong.

CHAPTER 17

WEBINAR NEWBIES

A great way to both build your audience and to develop your income is through the use of webinars. Perhaps we can get started with just outlining what a webinar is in the first place. It's basically just a seminar that is conducted over the web. There are many software options that you can use for this and most webinars will use screen-sharing, webcams or a combination of the two, along with possibly some real-time chat software. You'll usually have a certain subject that you're presenting on and then the audience can watch and interact with you.

Let's say that you are an expert on blogging and you want to provide an introductory webinar on how to get started with a blog. You might use this webinar to introduce people to the free WordPress platform and you could demonstrate, by way of real-time screen-sharing, how someone can install and configure WordPress from beginning to end. You can show how to set up the database, how to install a custom theme, how to activate plugins, how to write a blog post, how to insert images and so on. There's value there for people who want to learn how to use WordPress and these people are willing to pay for that kind of in-depth tutorial with real-time interaction.

Yes, it is true that webinars can take a lot of preparation, but what I can tell you is that the wards are also quite high. In fact, there are very few people that are willing to put in the time and effort to do webinars. Does this sound familiar? Just like there are people who are too scared to do videos, there are so many people who just don't want to do webinars. But you know what? That gives you the advantage, because now the competition is very low.

The fascinating thing is that your webinar can really take on all kinds of different formats and webinars can be positioned to suit all kinds of different goals and purposes.

I remember my first ever webinar was based around providing a lot of valuable information to the viewer so that they could go away and think to themselves, "You know what? I like that guy."

It was more about positioning myself as the expert in the niche and not just about creating a dollar. If you are doing webinars purely to make money, you are doing it wrong, particularly in the beginning anyway. It's always good to build your name and authority first, so people trust you. Then, you can pitch whatever you want.

The problem is nowadays everyone pitches something on a webinar, so the viewer is a lot smarter than what they used to be. Viewers have almost come to expect that just when the webinar starts, they'll probably hear the same usual opening, the same usual closing, and the same product pitch to encourage people to open up their wallets. They might be used to it, but that's not really the way I recommend you put together your webinar. You need to provide value first. You need to build your brand and your authority. Then, the viewer will want to buy from you, even if you don't put them through the hard sell.

If you do a webinar, I recommend you really look at what others are doing and change it around. Be unique, show that you care, and ask customers questions live in your webinar. After all, that's what webinars are meant to be for: to get everyone's feedback in real-time and in an open style conference setting. It allows your viewers to join you from anywhere in the world, as if you were all sitting around in the same conference room or event space. Really leverage the power of the Internet for that kind of real-time interaction and feedback.

So, by the time I got around to doing by fifth or so webinar, it was not unusual for me to be making $50,000. It's about building a strong brand, developing your audience, and really providing them with the value that they desire. If you find a good partner and product, you can usually instead of doing the webinar yourself and creating the product yourself, you might want to find someone who already has a product and experience in webinars to really do it. You would just host it and if they have an affiliate program, they could then use your affiliate link at the end of the webinar. That's how you'd get paid on the backend.

But how much money can you really make from a webinar? When there are so many different affiliate offers that you can promote by giving people a really good webinar, the income potential is positively astronomical. Let's run through some quick math to give you an idea of what is very reasonable and very possible.

Let's say that you've put together your own product of some kind and it sells for $997. You host a webinar where you talk about a relevant subject and the pitch is for this product. Let's say that you get 200 people on the webinar to watch you and then 10% of them follow through to buy the product. That's 20 people buying at $997, which works out to $19.940. I'd say that's pretty terrific for a webinar that might last about an hour. And that's not even including when you send out the webinar replay through your various channels and the long-term sales that you can generate over time. The rewards can be very, very high.

Even if you did the exact same webinar with 200 viewers, but you were promoting a $997 affiliate product with a 50% commission rate, you would still earn almost $10,000 from doing that webinar. There is some great income potential here without having to even have huge numbers of attendees. Getting 200 people on board is not that far-fetched, even for someone who is just starting out with affiliate marketing and webinars.

If you do a webinar with someone, just be sure that they are experienced in what they are doing and even ask around to see who else has had success partnering with them. The last thing you want is to send leads to someone else's webinar and they shave your leads and sales. There is a lot of shonky business going on in this industry. Trust me. If you don't know what you are getting into, they will eat you alive. Of course, it's always better to have your own product and pitch your own webinar, because it means that you are completely in control of all those moving parts. It also means that you are putting in more work to get it done, though.

When you're reading to run your own webinar, you'll find that there is a lot of software out there that you can use. If you're already on Google, using Google Hangouts is a possibility. This can tap into your existing list of contacts and it integrates very well with Google+. It's very easy to share links through this service too and it works great for collaborative efforts, so it's best for when you want to have more of a conversation with your viewers rather than a traditional presentation.

Another webinar option that you might want to try is AnyMeeting. The layout is very similar to GoToMeeting if you've ever used that, either as a presenter or as an attendee. What's great about AnyMeeting is that it is actually a free platform when you have up to 200 people watching. You do have to pay beyond that. The other downside is that the free webinar will have AnyMeeting advertising for the registration page, which may detract from your perceived professionalism. If you pay, then you can remove the ads. It is also limited in that only one presenter can talk at any one time, but this isn't a problem if you're the only host.

Some other popular webinar software includes WebEx, GoToWebinar, MegaMeeting, and FreeScreenSharing. When organizing and preparing your webinar, you should think about it in a similar way that you would think about doing a talk at a conference. You could prepare a PowerPoint presentation ahead of time and that's a great way to keep everything organized and on time. Again, this helps with building your brand image as a trusted authority and expert, and this will help with generating your sales both now and well into the future.

Remember that webinars are still just a tool. You have to use them appropriately if you want to achieve the desired effect.

CHAPTER 18

MONEY IS IN THE LIST

Let's say that you launch a product and you decide to sell it through a marketplace like Clickbank. Let's say that you actually do very well and make thousands of dollars from it. That's great, but this is very much a "hit and run" kind of mentality. The next time you launch a product, you almost have to start from scratch again, because you have no real way of reaching to those past customers or affiliates again. Even if you have a blog, people will come and go. They might forget about you and never return.

That's why people will tell you that the money is in the list. When you build up a strong mailing list, it means that you have this list of customers at your fingertips. Chances are that if they signed up for your list and bought one of your products before, these same people are pretty likely to buy something else from you at some point in the future, even if it's months or even years later. You have their e-mail. You can reach them, even if they haven't followed you on Twitter or visited your website in ages.

But, and this is a very big but, there is only going to be money in the list if you know how to milk the list. This is particularly true if you offer some sort of freebie gift for people who subscribe to your list. These people haven't yet demonstrated that they'll open up their wallets to you. So, there are a lot of sequences that you can then follow to get them into more of a buyer's mindset.

I usually do a series of follow-up emails set in my autoresponder after that initial freebie or gift. This way, after a certain number of days, they can get an e-mail about something that I learned or something that I could share with them that will help them in some way. This helps to build rapport and it helps them better respect me as an authority in my niche. They learn to trust me, because I am already providing value without asking for money from them. Then, eventually later on down the funnel, I will hit them up with something to buy, probably about the third or fourth email into the sequence. It's important to space these out over a period of time, so the subscriber doesn't get overwhelmed and opts out of your list before you have a chance to sell them on something.

On the other hand, if you are launching products and getting the affiliates to promote it for you, or if you doing straight media buys to a product that you are selling, then that is a completely different story. The person who opts into a list under those kinds of circumstances isn't just a tire-kicker who wants something for free; you have already created a buyer lead straight off the bat. And that can be a far better situation to be in.

For email marketing, you're going to want to use a reliable service that provides you with great list management tools. You also want to make sure that they can reliably send your mailouts at the time that you want them to and you want to make sure that they have a good track record of getting delivered properly.

Aweber is a very popular choice among email marketers, particularly because you can start your first month for only a dollar. You can choose from over 150 templates, it integrates well with WordPress and Paypal, and custom HTML is not a problem. There is no image hosting though.

Some of the other email marketing software services that should be on your radar are Constant Contact, MailChimp and InfusionSoft. They're all pretty big companies with good track records, especially MailChimp since there is a free option for you to get started. It's important that you go with a provider where you can review stats like the number of opens, clicks, unsubscribes, and complaints.

Let's get back to my own personal experience with this in the early days of my Internet marketing career. Back in the day before I launched products and when I was mostly making money from my blogs, I would generate subscribers through my following and also by dabbling in safe-swaps.com. Through these techniques, I built up a very good list and I was able to do it pretty quickly too.. In fact, I was able to grow my list to around 10,000 subscribers in about 6 months. For me back then, this was good. However, after I launched products, I then built up a list of 80,000 or so.

That all sounds pretty great and I was feeling really good about what I was able to accomplish, but there is one thing that you really need to understand about successful email marketing:

It's not really about the size of the list.

Instead, it's actually a lot more about the kind of relationship you are able to develop with your subscribers. It's far better to have a list of 1,000 people who are hanging on your every word and anxious to buy anything that you promote than it is to have a list of 10,000 people who just delete your messages and never buy anything.

Don't fall into the trap of just mailing out something for the hell of it. We are all tempted to do that, because we feel compelled to keep our mailing list active. We feel like we have to do something all the time, but that's not the case. Everything you send out should have a purpose. So, that's why it is better if you sit back and really spend the time to do things properly.

Review products, create bonus pages, do interviews and mail to those directly rather than just mailing to a sales page. Its best if you can mix these up each time you mail so you give your audience a variety of value.

One prime example of this is surveying your list members. You can use a service like Survey Monkey to handle that for you. They're really easy to use and they can provide some really powerful insights. You really get to know what the list members are like and what they want. This way, you can then put something in front of them that is far better suited for their particular tastes and needs. Your results will be that much better, because you took the time and effort to do something meaningful.

Another thing you can do is if you want to build up an email list as quickly as possible is to invest in solo ads. A solo ad is basically when you pay someone else to mail their list, on your behalf, encouraging their subscribers to head over to your opt-in page. In order to get set up with solo ads, then, you'll first need to create a squeeze page and have your leads get sent to there.

There are a lot of solo ad sellers that will charge you on a per-click basis. For example, you might find one that will sell you 500 clicks for about $150. Remember that the money is for 500 clicks and not for the number of opt-ins. You still need to have a strong squeeze page that converts. If you get 500 clicks, you might get about 200 that opt-in.

Then, the real action can happen. After they opt-in to your list, they can start buying the products that you are promoting either through the your thank you page for joining the list or buying after going through your autoresponder series. Whatever way they go, if you are getting 10% of those people to buy something, then you have 20 people buying your $97 product. Do a little quick math and you can see how you can very quickly make about $2,000. Do you see how the initial $150 investment in solo ads was totally worth it?

Another quick way to grow your list is through media buys and these work in pretty much the same way as solo ads. Find a network like Bing.com that offers very cheap clicks – usually around 20 cents per click, compared to the around 80 cents that Google would charge for the same. My point is if you can get cheap clicks to your squeeze page and you are getting highly relevant leads turning into buyers, then the results can be more than worth it. The media buys can be through all sorts of different ad networks, so it pays to play around with your keywords and to try different tactics until you find on that is really effective. Facebook advertising is also worth looking into and it can be a very cheap exercise if you take the time to test and tweak your campaigns.

Once you have that highly targeted email marketing list, you'll have the foundation to keep selling your products (or promoting affiliate products) for years to come. That's why they say the money is in the list.

CHAPTER 19

ONLINE SHOPPING WEBSITES

Another big way that you can make money on the web is through e-commerce. It makes a lot less sense today to open up a regular brick-and-mortar store, because there are so many other costs involved. You have to pay for rent and insurance and utilities and all the rest of it. That's why opening an online store where you have far less overhead just makes a lot more sense. And that means it puts more dollars in your back pocket.

In fact, I even started my own Internet career when I was a Power Seller on eBay way back in 2004. The great thing is that eBay is filled with anything you want to buy and I mean almost anything. That also means that you can sell just about anything too. Heck, you can even buy and sell cars on eBay. So, it's about way more than just fashion and random junk.

People spend billions of dollars online globally year after year and this number continues to rise. Online shopping is huge and it keeps growing. It's no secret that doing your business through an online store is totally the in-thing to do. It also means that you can literally tap into a worldwide marketplace and reach global customers.

When I was living in Thailand, I used to source and sell funny t-shirts. I set up a website called jokingtshirts.com and I was able to very well with that. There has been and always will be a market for funny shirts, and since I was already in southeast Asia, it was easy enough for me to source the shirts for a very good price.

It's actually not as complicated as you might think to set up your own online store. Even though most people still see WordPress as just some blogging software, it's actually a really powerful content management system that can be used for all sorts of different websites, including online stores.

All you have to do is install WordPress (which only takes

about five minutes) on your server, find or design the theme that you want to use, and invest in the shopping cart or e-commerce plugin or solution that you like. There are lots of them out there. WP e-Commerce is free and it's pretty popular. WooCommerce is another one and it comes from the same people who do WooThemes.

In fact, if you want to make things even easier, there are some hosting and full solution companies that cater specifically to this purpose. Some of the better known ones include Shopify, BigCommerce, and Volusion. They take care of everything, from hosting to design to taking care of the backend for inventory, orders, and shipping. It's really easy.

Selling things through eBay and through your own website can still be pretty profitable, but Amazon.com is nowadays the bigger supplier when it comes to selling online physical goods. The great thing about Amazon is that you can list your own products on there or promote other products.

They let third party retailers essentially set up online stores right through Amazon, which would be far more trusted by the average online shopper than some random website. And even if you don't have your products, you can promote other people's stuff and still make good money. Amazon really has grown a lot in the last few years.

If you are an affiliate and all you want to do is just promote other people's products, you can totally do that. Just go to the best sellers section and look at what's hot and what's good to promote. It's always a good idea to keep close tabs on what is going on sale too, because people are always looking for a bargain.

Then, just set up a WordPress site with the e-commerce features based on what you think you need, import the products from their site onto your site, and you're all done. There are some great WordPress solutions that work with datafeeds too, if you want to promote products that way.

To make money with Amazon, you just have to sign up for the

Amazon Associates program. That's basically their affiliate program and it usually starts out with a 4% commission rate, going up with volume. So, even in the beginning, if someone buys a $150 iPod, you earn $6 from that sale. The commission rate can go as high as 8.5% based on volume and, for certain product categories, the commission rate is fixed at an even higher rate.

For example, if you get people to buy Amazon Instant Video or game download products, you earn a 10% commission rate. If you get people to buy magazines, that's a 25% commission right now. And the best part is that you don't have to deal with any of the inventory or shipping yourself; you just have to send them the customers and Amazon takes care of the rest.

Another thing that you can try doing is to sign up as a drop shipper for some niche specific companies. What this means is that you don't have to manage any of the inventory yourself, because all of that is being handled by the actual company at their own warehouse.

What you do is set up your own online retail store and when you get a customer that buys something, the order and shipping information gets sent to the actual company for them to fulfill the order. You have far less startup costs and you don't have to deal with most of the fulfillment hassles. And you don't have to take out the warehouse space either.

Let's say, for example, that you decide you want to sell some adult toys. There are many sites that offer drop shipping services, so you can basically just create the site, use the XML feed that they give you, utilize the API to integrate it into your site, and before you know it, you have yourself a fully fledged adult toy site on the Internet.

Of course, if you don't want to sell adult toys, there are tons of other niches and industries that you can explore. Just put in the kind of stuff that you want to sell, followed by "dropshippers" in Google and take a look at the results. There are many of them.

Another option is to source a hot product that is selling online or at the store on Alibaba.com. The great thing about Alibaba is that they have products at ridiculously low prices infact it's a wholesaler, so something you would normally find at retail price online for $20 if you bought in 100 or 1000 lots would get it for around $1 each, the profit margin is huge if you are prepared to put in the work and buy and ship things yourself.

Pretty cool stuff right?

CHAPTER 20

THE SERVICE PROVIDER

When most people think about offering services on the Internet, they come at it from the perspective of being a one-man (or one-woman) operation. Let's say that you do graphic design and you want to help people design their websites, logos, banners and that kind of thing. You can make a lot of money doing this, but you are just one person. It's same with all sorts of other services that you can sell on the Internet, but who said that you have to do it on your own? If you go at it by yourself, you could be leaving a lot of money on the table, because you are really inhibiting your own earning potential.

When I had my office in Bangkok back in the day, I had 12 staff in that office offering search engine optimization (SEO) and Internet marketing (IM) services to local businesses. Companies paid us good money to help them get up in the rankings in search engines and they paid good money to help them get noticed, acquire customers and whatever else they wanted to achieve. The service industry is alive and well.

What I quickly found out, though, is that I really had to have the correct team in place in order to handle the orders. And even once I had the right team in place, I had to make sure that I was able to keep them occupied. Otherwise, I would be losing money by having them sit around and not really doing any real work. The jobs had to keep coming in and I had to make sure that my workers were being productive.

It's a real juggle to manage them and you will need to invest a lot of time in this, particularly in the beginning. Consider it an investment.

Once you get a solid team, the results can be incredibly huge. It may not be a surprise to you that offering services can be the most lucrative thing that you can do on the Internet. Yes, you can

My 3 Story Office in Bangkok, Thailand

make money with affiliate marketing, with blogging, or with e-commerce, but setting up an online services company where you are effectively outsourcing the work for not too much money can be very profitable. There are many overseas workers who are more than happy to work for less money than what you might have to pay someone in Australia, Europe or the United States.

The thing about offering services is that it isn't that hard for you to scale up as your business continues to grow too. You don't have to handle more inventory and you don't need more warehouse space. All you have to do after you build up that solid team is to grow it even bigger to handle the larger volume of orders that are coming through your digital doors. As your team gets bigger and bigger, you'll have yourself an unstoppable money-making army at your disposal.

Think about the greatest kings that have ever been. They all had huge armies. That's what running a massive brand and a big company are all about. You need to get out there to the masses and really start building your brand and, more importantly, really start attracting those customers.

Even if you start locally first, there is no reason with the technology we have available today why you cant go global. The Internet is vast and it's huge and it makes it so easy for you to reach anyone in any part of the world. That's true for members on your team, just as much as it is about the customers that you are trying to attract. You might live in New York, but there's no reason why you can't take on an SEO or IM client who happens to live in London, Prague or Melbourne. And just because you work out of San Francisco, that doesn't mean you can't have your team based somewhere else.

This is the greatest thing about having a website for your services. People can order online from anywhere in the world. You could be out having dinner with your wife, you could be sleeping, or you could even be on vacation, but your team is still hard at work. They're trained to handle those orders and keep your company up and running. They're trained to keep making you money, even if you are asleep.

It's not unusual to hire a team or to have virtual staff working for you from the Philippines, for example. Their English is very good and they are great with computers. You might also have a lot of luck building your team out of India, Pakistan, Thailand or all sorts of other places. The cost of living is a lot lower in these countries, but there are some very well-trained and smart people who work in IT in these countries. They'll have no problem tackling the work that you provide them.

If you are not sure about what services you want to offer, just go back to basics. It sounds simple enough, but really think of what it is that you think people need. Think about the problems that people have and then offer a solution. For me, I figured people needed websites for their companies and organizations, so what I did was I started up my online business where I could provide them with websites. I hired people to create them for a few hundred dollars and then I very easily turned around to sell the websites to local businesses for a few thousand dollars. You can see how doing this over and over again can prove to be incredibly profitable.

So, just think about what value you can bring to a customer. Think about what you can offer, create a services website, and take it from there.

ABOUT THE AUTHOR

Daniel Lew is an Internet Marketing professional / Entrepreneur who became a self made millionaire from doing what he loves the most making money online.

He has experience which varies from salesmanship right through to having his own internet marketing company offering services to local businesses, creating products and affiliate marketing. He is now an inspired Author, Coach and Speaker.

For more information on his products or to hire Daniel visit www.danlew.com or www.sevenfiguremarketer.net